DIVING
STATIONS

DIVING STATIONS

THE STORY OF CAPTAIN GEORGE HUNT
DSO* DSC* RN,
ONE OF THE MOST SUCCESSFUL ALLIED SUBMARINE
CAPTAINS IN THE SECOND WORLD WAR

PETER DORNAN

Pen & Sword
MARITIME

First published in Great Britain in 2010 by
Pen & Sword Maritime
An imprint of
Pen & Sword Books Ltd
47 Church Street
Barnsley
South Yorkshire
S70 2AS

ISBN 978 1 84884 321 9

Typeset by Acredula

Printed and bound in England
By the MPG Books Group

Pen & Sword Books Ltd incorporates the imprints of Pen & Sword Aviation,
Pen & Sword Family History, Pen & Sword Maritime, Pen & Sword Military,
Wharncliffe Local History, Pen & Sword Select, Pen & Sword Military Classics,
Leo Cooper, Remember When, Seaforth Publishing and Frontline Publishing.

For a complete list of Pen & Sword titles please contact
PEN & SWORD BOOKS LIMITED
47 Church Street, Barnsley, South Yorkshire, S70 2AS, England
E-mail: enquiries@pen-and-sword.co.uk

Website: www.pen-and-sword.co.uk

Contents

Acknowledgements

I wish to express my gratitude to a number of special people whose assistance in the preparation of this book was indispensable.

I would particularly like to thank former submariner Dr Michael White QC for his encouragement and mentorship while writing this story. Michael assisted in the acquisition of Captain Hunt's records from the Archivist, George Malcolmson, and the Director, Jeff Tall, of the RN Submarine Museum in Gosport, England. I am also grateful for Michael's assistance with the editorship of this book.

I am similarly grateful to Bob Milns AM, Emeritus Professor of Classics and Ancient History at the University of Queensland, for his assistance with the editorship.

I have relied heavily on the marvellous tome of Vice Admiral Sir Arthur Hezlet, *British and Allied Submarine Operations in World War II*, vol. 1. John Wingate's *The Fighting Tenth* was also very useful, as was *Supreme Gallantry* by Tony Spooner, the story of Malta's role in the Allied victory.

I would also like to thank Jan Wilson and former naval officer Richard Arundel for the suggestion that I write Captain Hunt's story.

I am particularly grateful to my patient personal assistants, Carol Jackson and Karen Twist, whose comments were always welcome. A special accolade goes to my wife Dimity, who was my chief support system and ready cheer squad when I felt the problems were getting too large.

I am especially grateful for the encouragement of the staff at Pen & Sword, especially my editors, Pamela Covey and Bobby Gainher.

Finally, I have to thank George Hunt for his patience, openness and willingness to share his unique experiences, to relive all that has passed and allow it to be witnessed by succeeding generations.

Peter Dornan

I dedicate this book to my grandson Kasper Argus Dornan

Peter Dornan

I dedicate this book to the Submariners who not only fight the enemy but also brave the dangers of the ocean depth.

George Hunt

Glossary

Aldis lamp	Hand lamp used for signalling.
Asdic (sonar)	The device by which submarines are detected by surface ships by transmitting sound waves into the water and identifying echoes. Submarines are also fitted with Asdics which are mainly used as listening hydrophones. When operated in the transmission mode, submarines could communicate with each other by Morse code (SST, Subsonic Transmission) or 'underwater telephone'.
Cant	Italian bomber.
Casing (fore- after-)	The upper 'deck' constructed above the pressure hull of the submarine to allow movement on it by crew. The casing is 'free-flood', i.e. allows water to pass through. At sea, the berthing wires are stowed beneath the casing.
CCR	Contact Control Rod: torpedo warhead pistol. The pistol in the torpedo warhead is activated by passing through the ship's magnetic field. Therefore it will activate by simply passing close under the ship or by hitting it.
CERA	Chief Engine Room Artificer.
Chariot	Two-man human torpedo.
Conning tower	(or bridge). The raised part in the centre of the submarine from which surfaced navigation is conducted. The only tenable part of her when on the surface, except for the casing.
Control room	The nerve-centre or control centre of the submarine.

DA	Director Angle: the amount of 'aim-off' when firing torpedoes required to allow for the course and speed of the target.
D/F	Direction Finding. Equipment for locating the bearing of a radio signal.
E-boat	(or 'MAS' for Italian). Term for German (or Italian) 35-knot motor torpedo or gunboat, or submarine chaser: length about 75 feet.
EO	Engineer Officer.
ERA	Engine Room Artificer.
Faithful Freddie	The magnetic compass used in emergency.
F-lighter	German 'flak', shallow-draught craft, often armed with an 88mm gun.
Fish	Torpedo (slang).
Folbot	Two-man collapsible canvas canoe.
FO(S) or FOSM	Flag officer (submarines).
Fruit machine	The calculating machine into which all relevant attack data is fed, and from which much of the necessary information is extracted to carry out a torpedo attack.
HE	Hydrophone Effect, i.e. propeller or engine noise heard by the sonar.
Heads	Lavatory and wash place.
HEDA	High Explosive Delayed Action.
Iron ring	A patrol line of several submarines established outside a port to catch the enemy.
Jimmy	Jimmy-the-One, Jim or Number One: First Lieutenant and Second-in-Command.
'Kipper'	(or 'Fish'). Torpedo (slang).
Main ballast tanks	The tanks which give the submarine its buoyancy. All are fitted with main vents; in the 'U-Class' No.1, MB was for'd; in No. 6, MB was aft.

Main vents	The large round valves on top of the main ballast tanks; operated by telemotor pressure or by hand. When the vents are opened, the air in the tanks escapes, allowing sea water to enter through the flooding holes at the bottom.
Night vision (or sight)	The ability to see in the dark. In most submarines it was customary for red lighting to be switched on in the control room and various compartments at least half an hour before surfacing at night. It was found that it takes twenty minutes for the eyes to adjust from normal lighting to darkness, thereby attaining true night sight: an essential requirement for lookouts.
Number One	First Lieutenant and Second-in-Command; the 'Jimmy'.
Outside ERA	The Engine Room Artificer whose place of duty is at the blowing panel in the control room. Being responsible for all auxiliary machinery 'outside' the engine room, he is also known as the 'Outside Wrecker'. He works the periscope hoist.
Panel	The conglomeration of valves and blows centralized in one position on the port side of the control room from which many valves and pumps are operated.
Perisher	Slang for Commanding Officers' Qualifying Course (COQC). The COs' Course was originally (circa 1905) started as 'The Periscope Course' in the Periscope School. The Periscope Course became 'The Perisher'.
Pilot	Slang for 'Navigator' (sometimes 'Vasco').
Planes	Slang for hydroplanes, the horizontal 'fins' which control the depth-keeping and angle of the submarine. Fitted fore and aft on each side of the pressure hull, they are operated by hydraulic oil pressure.
Port	The left-hand side of a ship facing the bow or forward. Called larboard in earlier times.

Q Tank	The emergency quick-diving tank situated forward. When flooded, the tank makes the submarine 10 tons heavier than her normal dived trim and bow heavy. In wartime, Q is always kept flooded when the submarine is on the surface ready for quick diving.
RNR	Royal Naval Reserve.
RNVR	Royal Naval Volunteer Reserve.
Sailing Orders	Instructions issued to a warship before going to sea; details of where to go, how to get there and what to do are set out.
SO	Senior Officer.
Starboard	The right-hand side of a ship as one faces the bow, or forward.
Stem	Bow part of the ship.
Stick	Slang for periscope.
SST	Subsonic Transmission for underwater communication.
Swept Channel	The channel swept clear of mines by minesweepers, to give safe passage to shipping.
TGM	Torpedo Gunner's Mate. The Petty Officer in charge of torpedoes and torpedo department.
Trim	The state of buoyancy when the submarine is submerged, i.e. light or heavy; bow up or bow down. A submarine is perfectly trimmed when it is level and when it dives, it has neutral buoyancy.
UJ-boat	(UB Jäger) German Anti-Submarine Escort Craft.
Watertight doors	The submarine is divided, in the U-Class, into watertight compartments by five bulkheads. Watertight doors are fitted into each bulkhead to provide crew access along the passageway but can withstand water pressure when closed.
W/T	Wireless Telegraphy.
Zigzagging	Steering from one side of the mean course to the other in order to confuse the aim of an enemy submarine.

Ranks in the Royal Navy

<u>Officers</u>
- Admiral of the Fleet
- Admiral
- Vice Admiral
- Rear Admiral
- Commodore
- Captain
- Commander
- Lieutenant Commander
- Lieutenant
- Sub Lieutenant
- Midshipman (Junior Officer)
- Cadet at Naval College or Training Ship

Chaplains and doctors are officers

<u>Ratings</u>
- Chief Petty Officer
- Petty Officer
- Leading Seaman
- Able Seaman
- Ordinary Seaman
- Boy Seaman
- Boy Seaman – at Naval College

In the Royal Navy, the Commanding Officer of a ship is known on board as the Captain, regardless of whether he is a Lieutenant, a Commander, a Captain or a Commodore.

The Captain of a ship (even a Lieutenant), therefore, is entitled to the normal acts of respect, such as being piped on board.

Rough comparison of officer ranks:
In the United Kingdom, the Royal Navy is the senior of the three services.

Royal Navy	*Army*	*Royal Air Force*
Rear Admiral	Major General	Air Vice-Marshal
Commodore	Brigadier	Air Commodore
Captain	Colonel	Group Captain
Commander	Lieutenant Colonel	Wing Commander
Lieutenant Commander	Major	Squadron Leader
Lieutenant	Captain	Flight Lieutenant

Measurements

This book is set during the Second World War. All measurements were then recorded using the Imperial System.

Rather than convert all measurements in the text to the metric system, this has only been done on a few occasions. The following is a relevant conversion chart.

METRIC-ENGLISH EQUIVALENTS

Metric Unit	English Equivalent
	Length
millimetre (mm)	0.03937 inch (in)
metre (m)	3.28 feet (ft)
kilometre (km)	.62 mile (ml)
	Area
square metre (m²)	10.76 square feet (ft²)
square kilometre (km²)	.386 square mile
hectare (ha)	2.47 acres
	Weight
gram (g)	0.035 ounce, avoirdupois (oz avdp)
gram	.0022 pound, avoirdupois (lb avdp)
tonne (t)	1.1 tons, short (2,000lb)
tonne	.98 ton, long (2.240lb)

Temperature

1 degree Celsius (1°C)   1.8 degrees Fahrenheit

Depth

Fathom   6 feet or 1.8 metres

Maps

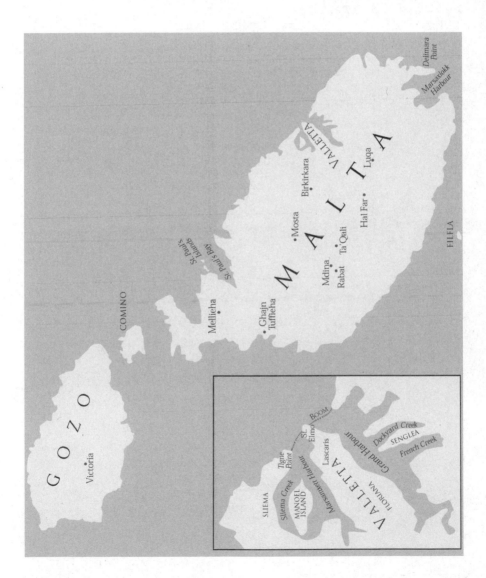

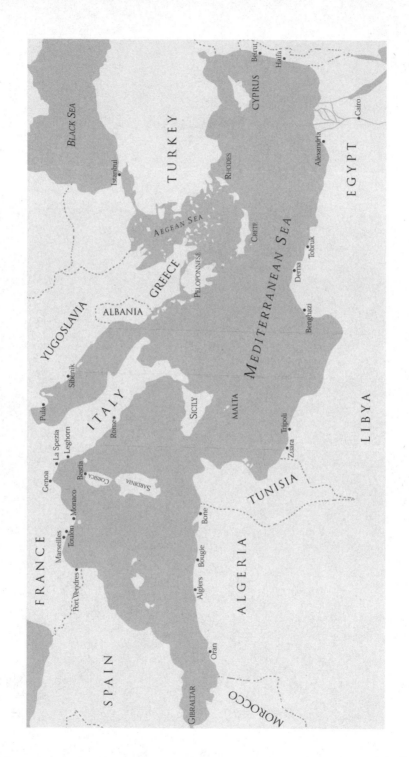

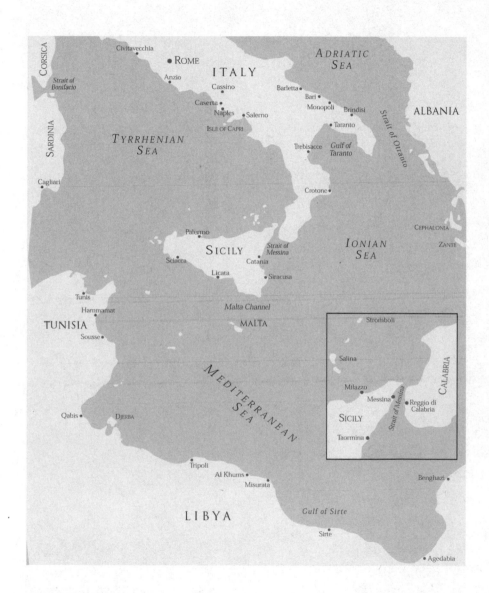

CORSICA

Civitavecchia

ROME

ITALY

Anzio

Cassino

Caserta

Naples

Salerno

ISLE OF CAPRI

SARDINIA

TYRRHENIAN
SEA

Cagliari

ADRIATIC
SEA

Barletta

Bari

Monopoli

Brindisi

Taranto

ALBANIA

Strait of
Bonifacio

Strait of Otranto

Trebisacce

Gulf of
Taranto

Crotone

CEPHALONIA

ZANTE

Palermo

SICILY

Strait of
Messina

IONIAN
SEA

Sciacca

Catania

Licata

Siracusa

Tunis

Malta Channel

Hammamat

MALTA

TUNISIA

Sousse

MEDITERRANEAN
SEA

Stromboli

Salina

Milazzo

Messina

Reggio di
Calabria

CALABRIA

Strait of Messina

Qabis

Djerba

SICILY

Taormina

Tripoli

Al Khums

Misurata

Benghazi

LIBYA

Gulf of Sirte

Sirte

Agedabia

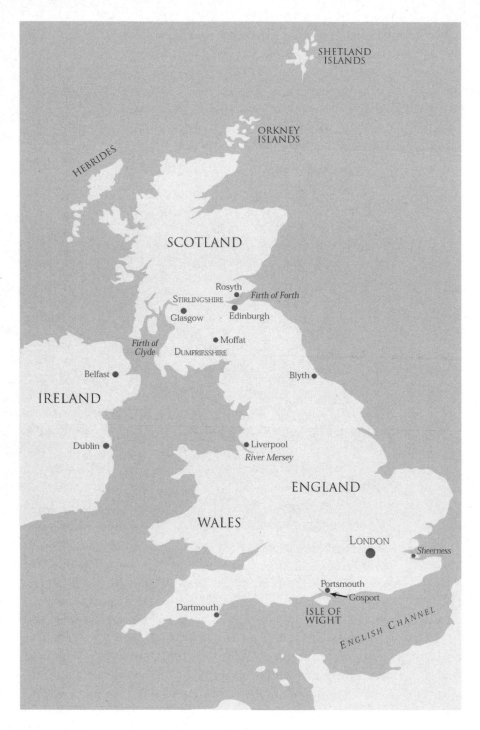

Prologue

29 April 1940. The North Sea, off the east coast of England. Evening, 7.00pm. A British submarine was silently sailing up the coastal swept channel, an area cleared of mines. A thick fog had developed, rolling in from the sea. Five men stood on the bridge, peering into the Stygian darkness. Survival depended on good eyesight and quick thinking. One was the Captain with two other officers and two men as lookouts.

The officers were anxious. The Captain, Lieutenant Frank J. Brooks, had already expressed his concern that they had not been given an escort, a destroyer or minesweeper, for protection and identification, particularly in view of the poor visibility they were now experiencing.

One of the two other officers, Lieutenant George Hunt, was the Navigation and Signals Officer. George looked every bit the seafaring man. He had a beard, which he kept neat and trimmed, his hair was very fair and his blue eyes were the same colour as the sea. He was lean and fit, and the ideal height for a submariner, 172cm (5'7½"). The other officer was Lieutenant John Trickey, a cheerful South African Reserve Officer, the Officer of the Watch. They shared the Captain's concern.

The submarine, HMS *Unity*, was one of the new breed of small submarines, Unity-class, or U-class. It was based at Blyth in Northumberland, a submarine base on the north-east coast of England. Earlier that day, before setting out, there had been some disruption as the regular Captain had suddenly been taken ill. An urgent replacement had been found, Lieutenant Brooks, and he had only arrived at Blyth at noon. Brooks quickly assumed command and the *Unity* sailed by 4.00 that afternoon.

Now, it would appear, they had every reason to be concerned. Due to an oversight in the Signal Distributing Office in Blyth, *Unity* was not told, before sailing, that she might meet a convoy coming down the swept channel from the north. U-class boats – a submariner refers to his 'boat' rather than his 'ship' – had three officers in addition to the Captain. The officers rotated watch four hours on and eight hours off. It was intense work being shared among George, Trickey and the First Lieutenant, Angus Low, the Second-in-Command, who was down below in the control room. (The Officers of the Watch (OOW) shared these duties, leaving the Captain free to plan and oversee everything. In stressful periods, such as now, he would be called to the bridge.)

The U-class submarines were launched in 1937. There were three of them at this stage – *Undine, Unity* and *Ursula* – the forerunners of sixteen ordered. Even though they were small, they were lethal, and had a crew of thirty-six. The vessel was 'diesel-electrically' driven. That is to say, the main power source while on the surface was derived from two effective 400hp Paxman diesel generators. They provided the power to charge the batteries (recharging was carried out on the surface – usually for a few hours at night) or to drive the two electric motors direct which turned the propeller shafts. In this way, the batteries could drive the ship whether on the surface or submerged.

These first three submarines were remarkable in appearance for their bulbous bows, housing two external torpedo tubes, but their main ability was to dive quickly, as little as sixteen seconds from surface to periscope depth.

The *Unity* was George's first operational submarine, which he had joined in April the previous year. As war became imminent, in June of the same year, 1939, King George held a review of the assembled Home Fleet, including the Reserve Fleet. On completion, all ships and submarines were dispersed to their prearranged war stations. When war was actually declared on 3 September 1939, the Royal Navy was on a war footing and highly organized.

On that fateful day, *Unity* was sitting off Heligoland, on Germany's doorstep, awaiting developments. (Heligoland was a fortified island which guarded the mouth of the Elbe River in Germany. From there, they could monitor shipping movements in and out of the river.) Since then, George had been on six patrols, mainly off the German coast and in the Skagerrak, the strait between Denmark and Norway.

George had experienced very little action at this stage, although he had regularly witnessed the terrible results of war, picking up survivors from ships sunk by the enemy. He had also dealt with the almost nightly bombing by the Germans, as Blyth was often hit.

This particular night, which was the start of George's seventh patrol, *Unity*'s orders were to proceed to a patrol area off Heligoland once again. George had just come up to the bridge to relieve Trickey on watch. Before actually relieving Trickey, through the fog and to the north, George could hear the eerie sounds of various sirens and foghorns heralding the presence of several ships in the channel. It was a little strange, as *Unity* had received no word of a convoy coming south. However, George's main concern as the Navigating Officer was hoping to sight a channel buoy in the vicinity, allowing them to make an alteration of course and remain safely in the channel.

A blast on a ship's siren was heard somewhere ahead, grabbing George's attention. At this point, the Captain took over control from the OOW. *Unity* replied with a long reply from her siren. That ship appeared close. Suddenly, a further blast was heard from another ship, even closer – too close. Like a spectre shrieking out of Hades, a dark shape reared out of the darkness and fog. It was a Norwegian merchant ship, the *Alte Jarl*, and it was on a near-collision course with *Unity*.

At this stage of the war, most people hardly knew what a submarine looked like, let alone whether it belonged to Germany or the Allies. As such, even though Norway was neutral, the captain of the *Alte Jarl* wasn't going to take a chance. He decided that a lone unescorted submarine had to be a German U-boat, and one less U-boat would be a good thing. He held his course and steered his ship hard over, aiming deliberately at the submarine. George stared as the

3

dark shape of the bow now raced directly towards him.

At the same instant, the Captain, standing next to him, reacted. Predicting the outcome, he ordered full speed astern both engines. He then told the OOW to sound three short blasts on the siren. The urgent penetrating wail shot out into the night. At the same time, he called down the voice pipe to the control room, 'Collision Stations! Shut watertight doors! Prepare to abandon ship!' This was quick thinking. The Captain knew the only way out of the submarine was up the conning tower – the crew should start moving now!

Then, at the last minute, as the *Alte Jarl* came towards its smaller target, the Norwegian captain realized the *Unity* was flying the British white ensign. The ensign, with a Union Jack in one corner and a red cross on it, caught what little light was reflected off the dense fog. Feverishly the Norwegian ordered full speed astern. The vessel responded, it began to slow, but it was too late. It continued charging towards *Unity*, its bow cutting through the water.

George braced himself. The bow of the Norwegian ship smashed into the side of the *Unity*, slicing her open. There was a terrible wrenching sound as metal ripped into metal. Initially, to most of the sailors, the full horror of the damage was muffled as the collision occurred underwater, forward of the bridge. However, the impact sent a sickening thud through the boat. Cutlery and crockery smashed and lights flashed out; men cursed. Bitterly cold sea water raced in. Within moments, the whole of the fore end of the submarine was flooded. The boat was certainly going to sink.

Down below, there appeared to be little panic. Men were well trained for this type of emergency and followed their drills. There was, of course, a keen sense of urgency, but everybody followed a procedure and a job. Any outward fears that they may forever be entombed in this metal coffin were only reflected in their wide eyes. Here, in these dark, confined spaces, the First Lieutenant, Angus Low, organized and calmed the men. He then urged those in the control room to scramble up the conning tower ladder where they were met by George at the top on the bridge, having been stationed there by the Captain.

As they reached the bridge, George ran a quick eye over each man to make sure they were alright and that they had secured their lifebelts. The lifebelts were a problem. They were designed only as a rubber tube which circled the chest with a connecting hose to allow the tube to be blown up by mouth. If they were inflated before going up the conning tower, it could be difficult to get through the upper hatch onto the bridge. As well, it was ridiculous that the bunting which covered the tube, of all the colours to choose, was dark blue – a colour not easily discernable at night in a black sea. George marvelled at the lack of foresight by his seniors responsible for such decisions.

As men fumbled in the dark with their lifebelts, George organized them to gather on the after-casing of the hull and to wait there until they either got washed off or the boat sank. The ship was already at an angle with the bow under the water. One man approached George and insisted, 'I need to get back down there and help.' George looked at him incredulously, wondering whether he was genuinely brave or a 'twit' – it was very obvious it was impossible to go down the conning tower as there was only room for men coming up.

They were running out of time. Two men still hadn't come up and the submarine was sinking fast. Angus Low remained down below in charge and Able Seaman Henry Miller had been operating the motors. His desperate job was to cut off the motors to stop the propellers. If the submarine sank, the spinning propellers could do a great deal of damage to men in the water.

Lieutenant Trickey and George stayed on the bridge with the Captain until everybody except Low and Miller had climbed out.

There was a procedure, if the submarine is sunk and lying on the bottom, which made it possible to escape by deliberately flooding a compartment which was fitted with a twill (tough denim) trunk. This allowed air to be trapped to enable a man to get out through a hatch in the torpedo stowage compartment, or the engine room compartment. However, the torpedo stowage compartment had been directly hit by the *Alte Jarl* and was flooded already rendering it useless for escape, which left the engine room. There was also a third avenue of escape and that was the conning tower. At this stage, the

Captain ordered George to shut the upper conning tower hatch and stand on it. He called for him to stay there until, as the *Unity* sank, water pressure would take over and keep the hatch shut.

This was good thinking by the Captain as it would have the effect of preventing the conning tower and the control room from being flooded, thus leaving Low and Miller one final sporting chance to escape. Unfortunately, by staying on the bridge, as the stricken vessel dropped into the deep, George and the other two officers would be exposed to the full force of the resulting suction.

Slowly at first, George felt the boat steadily sink beneath him. He kept his feet firmly planted on the now receding conning tower hatch. Initially, the cold shocked him. The water quickly swirled around his legs and then lapped higher, grabbing at his chest. Then suddenly there was no more time. The submarine with the three officers on the bridge slipped away and speared straight down. The sailors waiting on the casing plunged into the water. Men cursed again. Fortunately most of them managed to swim reasonably clear of the suction.

The water was dark and unpredictable. George had barely caught his breath when suddenly he was aware of a tremendous unseen force dragging him under, sucking him away from the surface and precious oxygen. The sea closed over and rumbled above him. Like a rag doll, he was swirled into the vortex created by the submarine as it sank into its death dive. He had barely managed to grab a lungful of air and desperately held his breath. He must stay calm and concentrated. As the submarine below him picked up speed, the turbulence twisted and rolled him and he fought for stability.

He was sinking fast – 20, 30 feet. He must not panic now. His resolve was strengthened by the knowledge that they were in a 100-foot deep channel; this was as deep as he could be dragged. He had been through the escape drills in basic training at Fort Blockhouse at Portsmouth in the underwater escape chamber, but nothing had quite prepared him for this. If he remained conscious, he might be able to survive.

He dropped further into the abyss – 70, 80, 90 feet. His lungs felt as if they were being crushed. The pressure was increasing rapidly and he was hurting. Then suddenly, he was aware of a developing pain in his ears. Damn. He had dropped so fast, he had not been able to clear his ears – to equalize the pressure. He felt a searing pain in both his eardrums as they perforated. He felt like yelling, but resisted the urge.

When would it stop . . .?

CHAPTER ONE

The Early Years

'Wouldst thou' – so the helmsman answered –
'Learn the secret of the sea?'
Only those who brave its dangers
Comprehend its mystery.

Henry Wadsworth Longfellow 1807–1882

George had always treasured the idea of going to sea. Even as a 12-year-old, while still at preparatory school, he imagined himself as the Captain of his own ship standing on the bridge. He was fortunate in that he came from a unique background which was able to nurture these dreams. He had a strong Scottish heritage with links to the sea: his great-grandfather (also George Edward) had been a shipbuilder in Glasgow. His formative years had also stimulated in him a sense of adventure and independence, qualities necessary for embracing life on the ocean wave. The period of history he was born into was also providential.

In the early half of the twentieth century, Britain was riding the crest of her empire-building policies. The map of the world was splashed with red, bristling with dozens of 'Outposts of Empire'. It was a time of expansion, opportunity and adventure. In this era, Britain exported her bloodlines all over the world to maintain her colonies. George's family was a microcosm of this excitement: his three uncles were posted to India, Canada and the Sudan. Fired by a similar impulse, George's father, John Hunt, a chartered accountant, joined the Colonial Service and was appointed to the British Protectorate of Uganda.

In 1913, George's father married his mother Emily, a nurse, in Kampala, the capital of Uganda. Tragically, their early happiness was marred as their first child Ellenora, who was born in 1914, died in February 1916. Consequently Emily, who was at this stage pregnant with George, was sent back to Scotland in order to have access to better medical facilities and support. Like many of his forefathers, George was born there, at Milton of Campsie, the family's ancestral home in Stirlingshire, not far from Glasgow, on 4 July 1916. (George's grandfather, also John Hunt, had founded the Calico Printing works there.) He was christened George Edward Hunt.

As soon as his mother was well enough to travel, she embarked on a remarkable journey, unaccompanied and with her infant son, to be united with her husband in Uganda. Apart from anything else, George had been born right in the middle of the First World War. Furthermore, the winding down of the Gallipoli campaign had meant that normal passenger ships were not yet running in the Mediterranean and Suez Canal. Accordingly, the courageous Emily had to go from Britain to Mombasa the long way, right around via Cape Town and then up the east coast of Africa. Because of the predatorial German U-boats, ships that were sailing from Britain to South Africa had to be protected in convoys. The speed of a convoy is governed by the average agreed speed of the slower ships and so it took two and a half weeks to reach Cape Town.

Here she had to disembark and negotiate her onward journey to Mombasa. It took four days to arrange passage to join a ship going up the east coast, but a week later she disembarked at Mombasa. Emily, and of course George, had so far been travelling for some four weeks. Now, to reach the next destination, she was faced with an uncomfortable and hot journey. They were almost on the Equator and the distance to Nairobi was some 1,250 kilometres, rising to over 2,000 metres. Fortunately, some of it was by train, as the railway from Mombasa to Nairobi in Kenya had just been completed.

Here, in Nairobi, Emily spent three days during which she managed to arrange the final leg of the journey. The railway line was still building its painful way upwards towards Uganda. (Indeed it was not finally connected between Kampala and Mombasa until 1931.) Accordingly, Emily opted for road transport and a bus (of sorts) took Emily and George, still all in one piece, to Kampala and a very relieved husband.

It should be mentioned, however, that they were not entirely entering the 'great unknown'. Emily had already experienced a variation of this adventure in 1913 to be married, but then she had been accompanied by a friend. Also they had sailed through the Mediterranean and the Suez Canal, which had been very different.

George's earliest memories were of a relaxed and privileged life, complete with housekeepers and nannies. Even though he mixed with children of other ex-patriots, his closest playmate was Mbote, the gardener's son, and he was fondly looked after by a black nurse. His existence was generally carefree, allowing time for imagination and adventure, but the situation and culture of the times did not allow him to develop any close experiences or warm memories of his parents. In fact, he found his father to be a rather strict disciplinarian, a trait which kept him distant.

At the age of 5, George started attending a little Dames (Early Childhood) school in Kampala. However, as it was traditional for British citizens in the colonies to send their children back to Britain for education, at 7 and a half, George was escorted to London by sea with the wife of the Bishop who was going on leave. Unfortunately, he was not to see his father again. George's separation from his parents was one of the almost inevitable drawbacks, so far as families were concerned, of Britain's vast colonial influence.

The ocean voyage was a different and interesting experience in itself, as was the land journey. From London, George was put on a train and placed in the charge of the guard in his van. George spent the entire journey in the van. He had a luggage label attached to his shirt, highlighting his destination: 'Moffat, Scotland'. The guard was very good-natured, but teased, 'I may have to throw you out if necessary.' He was met at Moffat in Dumfriesshire by his father's sisters, two doting aunts, and was then placed in boarding school at St Ninian's Preparatory School in Moffat.

St Ninian's, although generally comfortable, had elements of a Spartan existence. Kilts were worn as part of their best uniform, for church etc. There were sixty boys in attendance and they would begin the day with a cold shower, then start 'prep' at 7.00am before breakfast. After lunch, which finished at 1.30pm, the boys were required to be outdoors, where George revelled in playing golf, fishing, skating or rugby, depending on the season and school activities. From 5.30 to 6.30pm, there was further school work or 'prep' before supper. Overall, George coped well with this life, the discipline and routine preparing him for later institutional living and heightening his sense of independence.

George remained at St Ninian's until he was 13 and a half. During this seminal period, there were other events that helped to forge his character. Firstly, he was influenced by his uncle, George, his father's brother, who had just retired after serving as a civil engineer in what was then known as the British Sudan Civil Service in Khartoum in the Sudan. During holidays, the uncle spent much time with George, teaching him fly-tying, fishing and golf. With his aunt, the family often went camping in their caravan, fishing for trout or salmon, pitching their tent and living in the wilderness. His uncle and aunt became much loved by George – a surrogate mother and father and a wonderful influence on his life.

The other great impact was his cousin, Ian Arthur. The boys were the same age and they quickly formed a strong brotherhood. At about 10 years, they joined the Boy Scouts Association, an organization that challenged and satisfied their adventurous spirits. As well as the skills, values and concepts they acquired here, during the holidays, the boys would regularly hike for kilometres, tramping over the hills, often through snow, their kilts swishing around their knees.

As their confidence grew, they would jump on their bikes and ride off in the holidays touring all over Scotland. Many times, George would go by himself where he would camp out and fish – in fine weather, or foul – even snow. Occasionally, when he called at a farm, he would beg for milk and eggs. Some of the wives would say, – Och, y-dinna want to be camping outside with this weather. Come awa ben and sleep in the loft – an offer too difficult to refuse.

When he was 12 and a 'senior' boy, he would enjoy going to the Headmaster's study in the evenings where the Headmaster would read books to him and the other seniors, an activity which stimulated adventure – *Jock of the Bushfeld, White Fang, Moby Dick* and the like. He would also talk to the boys and discuss life generally, their hopes and future careers. To George, he was a wonderful man.

George also found he was interested in things mechanical. With advice and some assistance from one of the masters, 'Jimmy' Black, he made a wireless set, complete with crystal and 'cat's whiskers', wire that grated on the crystal to complete the circuit. With great excitement, he received London: 'This is 2LO calling.'

By the time he was 12, he had firmly crystallized the idea that he would like to go to sea. Britain, at this stage, was expanding its maritime strength. Indeed the British Merchant Fleet was larger than the rest of the world's fleets combined. From prep school, it was possible to attend one of the three main seafaring training colleges which would prepare a boy as an officer for either the Merchant Navy or the Royal Navy: HMS *Conway*, HMS *Worcester* or the Nautical College at Pangbourne. Or he could enter straight into the Royal Navy through the college at Dartmouth.

At 13 and a half, in January 1930, George passed the entrance examinations and entered HMS *Conway* as an officer cadet RNR (Royal Naval Reserve). This would give him an opportunity to train for both careers in maritime life.

For a boy interested in going to sea, HMS *Conway* was about as desirable as it gets. The *Conway* had a long naval tradition going back to 1859, not so long after Nelson's victory at Trafalgar. After that monumental sea battle, the Admiralty became fully aware of the benefits, indeed the necessity, of training young officers for the sea. When approached by the Mercantile Marine Service Association, the Admiralty offered HMS *Conway*, a frigate that had recently returned from the Far East.

In 1876, as demands grew, HMS *Nile*, recently returned from the West Indies, eventually took over training duties. The *Nile* was a beautiful three-masted, 92-gun battleship. After being refitted out for her new duties, she was renamed HMS *Conway* and moored off Rock

Ferry Pier on the River Mersey, just up from Liverpool. This was to be George's home for the next three years. He thought she was splendid.

While George was proud of his new uniform, it was the first time he had ever worn long trousers. For comfort, he thought they compared unfavourably with his kilt.

The boys, about 100 of them, slept in hammocks with all their worldly possessions stored in a sea chest under their hammock. George quickly adapted to the conditions and managed to thrive on the challenges. Even though this situation allowed the boys to learn 'hands-on' about the way of life at sea, they attended normal class lessons on board, with the addition, of course, of extra maritime subjects, such as navigation, engineering, seamanship and ship construction.

They were also able to take part in land-based activities. The Admiralty owned several acres of sporting facilities at Rock Ferry and the boys played rugby and other sports. These included rowing and sailing in dinghies and cutters. In the nearby swimming baths, George was able to improve his swimming and eventually took and passed the Life Saving Exams, set by the Royal Humane Lifesaving Society.

While here George was able to capitalize on his athletic abilities when he became captain of an unbeaten rugby team, playing scrum half and taking over the role as kicker. At the end of the season, his emerging leadership qualities were recognised when he was presented by Captain Richardson with a silver cup, inscribed: 'To G.E. Hunt – in appreciation of his Captaincy of an unbeaten Bantams Fifteen. Dec 1931. Played 12 won 12'.

George also enjoyed rowing. He delighted in watching the annual regatta as crews from *Conway* raced against crews from HMS *Worcester*, a rival training ship. This event had become an annual competition from 1890 and was always a highlight for the boys, as was the annual rugby match against the Nautical College at Pangbourne. This was played on the Birmingham University rugby ground, neutral territory halfway between HMS *Conway* and Pangbourne.

George graduated from HMS *Conway* as a Senior Cadet Captain in August 1932, with a nomination to Midshipman, Royal Naval Reserve. He was seldom actually 'top of his class' at school work, although once he got to sea and embarked on his chosen career, he passed all his examinations in a very satisfactory manner.

In those days, the Admiralty looked at Britain's seaborne trade and its defence from the larger Empire perspective. Britain had dozens of colonies which needed servicing, encouraging the growth of a plethora of Merchant Navy shipping companies. Such was the demand that one company alone, the Blue Funnel Line, Alfred Holt and Company, had 110 ships.

So at 16, as an indentured cadet, George started his apprenticeship in the Merchant Navy, joining the Scottish Company of 'Paddy' Henderson. The Henderson Line sailed mainly to India and Burma, presenting to George, or any young British sailor, a heady introduction to a life at sea – a chance to visit 'the far-flung outposts of Empire'. From another aspect, George very quickly became aware of the tremendous strength of Britain's Merchant Fleet and the extent of the influence of Britain in world affairs.

There were four cadets allotted to George's first ship, one attached to each of the three officers and the fourth on day work. The cadets mainly learned by understudying the officers and being given 'hands-on' navigation and seamanship instruction. From all aspects, George's learning curve was about to accelerate. The theory learned in HMS *Conway* was now being put into practice.

Each cadet sat for an examination every four months, the papers being set by the School of Navigation in the Royal Technical College in Glasgow. (The College was soon to become the University of Strathclyde but retained a very strong maritime department.) But George was also on the brink of learning about trade, business and tolerance for different races and cultures. One of the many tasks of the Henderson Line was to deliver coal and other supplies to the many British bunkering and maintenance stations established throughout the world.

This was at a time when ships worldwide were slowly converting from sail to steam, requiring coal for hungry steam engines. George's first ship was the SS *Arracan* which was crewed by Indians with British officers. On his first voyage, the ship transported coal from Methil, in Scotland, and then discharged it at Perim Island, a British possession in the Middle East, where the Red Sea flows into the Gulf of Aden. This generated much interest for George – not only in negotiating the Suez Canal and travelling through the Red Sea, but in experiencing Arab and Muslim culture.

Unloading the coal was a slow, hard, primitive business and entailed a gang of natives in the hold shovelling the coal into bags before hoisting the bags in slings out of the hold. They then sailed on to Aden, the capital of Yemen, two days away, by which time the holds would have been meticulously cleaned, allowing them to take on salt. When the holds were full, George was intrigued to see that the salt was flattened and stamped with a huge carved wooden 'stamp' with an effigy of a royal crown on it – to deter theft. This cargo was taken to Bombay, across the Arabian Sea. From Bombay, the ship sailed up to Karachi, which, at that time, was still in India. Here, they would load some general cargo for Colombo in Ceylon (Sri Lanka) and then on to Calcutta in India.

Calcutta was full of interest to George, especially as his cousin Ian Arthur's uncle, Sir Charles Arthur, was there. Apart from his business interests, Sir Charles was the Honorary Colonel of the Calcutta Light Horse and took George to dine at the Calcutta Club. This allowed George an insight into the sumptuous life led by the Burra Sahibs (men) and the Mem Sahibs (women) in the days of the British Raj.

While at Calcutta, George experienced a large earthquake which shook the whole region as far as Rangoon in Burma. The earthquake undoubtedly increased the size and strength of the normal bores (walls of water), for which the Hooghli is famous, into a miniature tsunami sweeping upstream from the Ganges Delta. A large German ship moored downstream of the *Arracan* broke adrift from its moorings and was forced up the river, finally crashing into the Howrah Bridge. The Howrah Bridge was then a floating structure of linked pontoons and was the only method by which vehicular traffic could get from the main city of Calcutta across the river to its railway station. The ship smashed into the bridge packed with people, severed all its moorings and carried it away upriver.

Even though George was often confronted by scenes of abject poverty in Calcutta, he also noted there was great beauty and colour reflected in the clothes, jewels, architecture and market places. Indian culture and its mode of living, and Hinduism, were so different to his own. It was not hard to ponder why India had been a source of wonder and inspiration for philosophers and poets since ancient times. India was, after all, Britain's 'Jewel in the Crown'.

The *Arracan* continued on to Burma where the ship moored at Rangoon. Here, the boys visited the famous Shwedagon Pagoda. Rarely had George witnessed such an exotic and impressive sight. The Pagoda, a monument to Buddha, glittered breathtakingly in the tropical sun. Imposing at over 120 feet in height, it was rumoured to have been inlaid with thousands of diamonds, rubies and sapphires. At the very pinnacle, there was supposed to be a single, magnificent 76-carat diamond.

George was informed that the recent earthquake he experienced in Calcutta had also shaken the Pagoda and several of the jewels were said to have fallen into the streets. He was warned the peddlers were selling bits of glass, offering them as jewels, 'Jewels from the Pagoda, Sahib!' Here also, as George witnessed hundreds of locals praying in the Pagoda, the complex radiated a palpable sense of beauty and serenity.

From Rangoon, the ship moved on to Bassein and Moulmein (both in Burma), where rice and bran were loaded into the holds. While crossing the Indian Ocean en route to Mauritius, where they were to load sugar and peanuts, there was a moment of tension. A fire had started smouldering in one of the holds due to spontaneous combustion of the bran – the hold was quickly completely sealed, thus killing the fire. They had been lucky.

Homeward bound after Mauritius, George witnessed one of the most breathtaking sights on the ocean when they passed the *Passat*, one of the Erickson Line's sailing ships. The *Passat* was one of the last of the grand four-masted barques still working. She was under full sail with the wind behind her, racing like an express train as she scythed through the aquamarine waters in front of him. She was stunning!

The following year, 1933, George was appointed the senior cadet in the brand new SS *Henzada*. This ship sailed on past India around the Bay of Bengal to Burma, and docked at Rangoon. At Rangoon, with the Captain's blessing, George and one of the other cadets seized an opportunity to travel right up the mighty Irrawaddy to Mandalay. The Henderson Line owned five river steamers, the Irrawaddy Flotilla, and operated them as a community service. It took about three days to travel the 400 miles (640 kilometres), stopping at many villages upstream. Every bend in the river was an adventure. Natives eking out a primitive existence would paddle alongside, then jump on deck and barter their produce.

At the end of each voyage, George continued his midshipman studies and sat for examinations. In 1935, as part of his training, he joined his first naval vessel, HMS *Achilles*, a light cruiser boasting twelve 6-inch guns; the Captain was Colin Cantlie, a submariner from the First World War. He was a charismatic type of character who never wasted an opportunity to influence the midshipmen in all things naval, but particularly in relation to pursuing a career in submarines.

This seafaring experience was decidedly different to Merchant Navy life. George devoured the naval traditions and Captain Cantlie regularly challenged the midshipmen. He would trap a couple of unsuspecting boys with 'You will have breakfast with me tomorrow before "colours"' – a sign to be alert. ('Colours' was the tradition where the colours, the RN white ensign, was hoisted at 8.00am, while the Royal Marine band played 'God Save the King'.) The next morning at breakfast, the Captain would regale the midshipmen with interesting naval details and trivia. He also encouraged debate on all subjects and questioned them relentlessly. The occasion inevitably served to stimulate (brainwash) the boys concerning the benefits of becoming a submariner. (Out of a gunroom of eight midshipmen, it was hardly surprising that five of them ultimately volunteered for and qualified in submarines.)

George was also introduced to the excitement of conflict. The ship normally carried an Osprey reconnaissance seaplane, with a pilot in the front and another position behind him for either a gunner with a Lewis machine gun or a telegraphist to stand in, being anchored with a belt around his waist and hooked to the floor. Three times, George found himself in this position.

The plane was launched off the ship from a 20-metre-long catapult. This produced a tremendous thrust as it was fired by a cordite charge, an event which was exciting in itself. However, George's function was to lean out of the plane and operate a winch to tow a windsock behind which would serve as a target for anti-aircraft guns of the fleet. As the guns opened up, George felt the adrenalin pump through his chest..

One of the events which impressed George tremendously was the Jubilee Review on 16 July 1935. For hundreds of years, the Admiralty treasured a tradition where the Monarch reviews the massed ships of the Royal Navy. That year, the event was held in the Solent, a wide channel off Southern England (Hampshire) between Portsmouth and the Isle of Wight. The occasion generally served to showcase the power and size of the British Navy. This time, it was also to celebrate the Silver Jubilee of HRH King George V and an overwhelming fleet of 160 warships took part in the review.

Everywhere George looked there were ships from one horizon to the other. After lunch, the Royal yacht *Victoria and Albert* sailed past in review while the King took the salute on the bridge. All sailors 'fell in' (stood to attention) on the deck lining the side of each ship. It was grand theatre and an impressive ceremony as each ship cheered while the King sailed past flying his standard, and later the flag signal for 'splice the mainbrace'. ('Splice the mainbrace' is an order to issue the crew with a drink – an extra tot of rum or grog. The phrase is a mainstay of pirate vernacular in popular culture.) However, midshipmen were not allowed to drink spirits, so George drank the King's health in lemonade.

The following day the whole fleet put to sea, the King in his flagship, HMS *Nelson* – an extraordinarily impressive sight. HMS *Achilles* had on board (specially for this occasion) a small radio-controlled aircraft about the size of a Tiger Moth or Cessna, called a Queen Bee. This was shot off from the catapult and then flown over the fleet. Ships fired live shells at it in a fine display of anti-aircraft firepower and in due course it was shot down. George was put in charge of a cutter to retrieve the remains still floating.

In the afternoon there was a demonstration to exercise the big guns. HMS *Centurion*, an elderly battleship, had been painstakingly fitted out to be fully radio-controlled, with not a soul on board; she was then fired at by the fleet. The attacking battleships, however, had their big 15- and 16-inch guns fitted with sub-calibre sleeves. This saved the expense of hurling an enormous 15-inch projectile, as the actual shell which winged its way towards the *Centurion* was perhaps only 4-inch.

It was all very dramatic and the King, who, after all, was a naval officer himself, no doubt thoroughly enjoyed the day. (Surprisingly, after all this bombardment, the *Centurion* did not sink. She was finally used, many years later, as part of a breakwater for the 'Mulberry' harbour used by ships of the Allied invasion off the Normandy beaches of northern France in June 1944.)

There was one further interesting experience for George during the shoot. He was sent to watch the 1935 version of the 'computer', then called the 'Fire Control Table', a table roughly 8 feet square situated in the bowels of the ship that contained masses of valves and Meccano. Round the table stood some eight Royal Marines (bandsmen actually). They operated little wheels feeding information into the machine such as enemy course, range, own course and speed, temperature, type of shell, fuse etc. This information was 'computed' and fed away to the guns which were, in some cases, automatically laid and trained, and fuses set. To George it was fascinating.

Meanwhile, across the Channel, another nation was also sabre-rattling, setting in motion a chain of events that would eventually collide with George's world. Two months after the Jubilee Review, on 15 September 1935, Germany celebrated a 'Rally of Freedom' at the Nuremberg Congress. This referred to the provocative re-introduction of compulsory military service and the 'liberation' from the Treaty of Versailles, the agreement signed at the end of the First World War forbidding Germany to have a defence force. There was also a more sinister agenda as the Congress voted to deprive the

Jewry of citizenship and adopted a new national flag, the Nazi swastika, an emblem that would forever remain one of the most powerful symbols of odium and cruelty.

In 1936, George went back to Glasgow to study for his Second Mate's Certificate – to become a watchkeeping officer. He attended the Royal Technical College, then undergoing transition to the University of Strathclyde, and lived in digs not far from there. This situation allowed him a more stable social life.

He befriended a South African from Kimberley, Joe Abrahams, who was studying to become a civil engineer. Joe and George both played rugby for the College – like George, Joe had an adventurous streak. With George and Ian Arthur, the three of them would camp out over the hills above the valley of the Moffat Water and Loch of the Lowes. They would also go sailing together. Often they would charter a 4-ton sloop and cruise in the Firth of Clyde and its many lochs.

One particular social event stood out, however, which was to shape the rest of his life. This was called a university 'rag'. Students dressed up, wore official badges and were given a tin with a slot in it. The aim was to relieve the public of their monies as the tin was rattled in front of them. All over Glasgow students collected vast sums of money for the hospital charities.

George had done well for the morning and boarded the top deck of a tram in order to return to his digs. To his delight, he found two beautiful young ladies sitting in front of him. He became interested when he overheard them arguing about the amount of money the students had raised that day, so, seizing the opportunity, he interrupted the conversation.

'Excuse me,' he said, 'I've just come from the City Hall where a friend of mine is at the receiving end, counting of the money boxes, and he tells me we've collected much more than that.'

'Really?' the women said, now paying attention. The ice was broken. George took the advantage and prattled on. Fortunately for him, they all got off at the same tram stop. One young lady went in one direction and the one George was interested in went his way. She was, in fact, living in the same crescent as him. (The crescent consisted of a row of houses, three storeys high, like terraced houses, with big gardens in the front of them.)

George continued the conversation on the way back. She introduced herself as Phoebe Silson and she was studying physiotherapy at the University of Glasgow. He found out her Scottish grandparents had settled in Kimberley in the Cape Colony of South Africa in 1880 where she had been born. After she had matriculated, she had come to Scotland to attend an old established teaching hospital, the Western Infirmary, linked to the University.

In an effort to get closer, George tried a long shot. 'Do you know Joe Abrahams?' he asked, referring to his friend from Kimberley in South Africa.

'Yes, of course,' she replied.

Amazingly, Joe was a family friend. In fact, Phoebe's parents had asked him to keep his eye out for her as she didn't know many people in Glasgow.

This turned out to work well for George and he began courting her.

In mid-1936 George passed the examination for his Second Mate's Certificate, which he proudly received on his 20th birthday, 4 July. His Uncle George presented him with a beautiful sextant, with his congratulations. Now a junior watchkeeping officer and feeling pretty pleased with himself, he rejoined the Merchant Navy, securing a position with Alfred Holt and Company – the Blue Funnel Line. This company was huge and owned much of Hong Kong on the Kowloon side, including most of the waterfront. This commission enabled him to visit the Far East and continue his adventures.

His first ship was the *Laomedon*, and he sailed to French Indo-China, Dutch East Indies, Hong Kong, Japan and China. Every port was different and exciting, but one memorable event occurred in Shanghai. Because he was also a junior officer in the Royal Naval Reserve, he was invited to spend six days in HMS *Bee*, one of the RN gunboats. These vessels patrolled the Yangtze River, keeping an eye on British interests there and this allowed him to sail up the Yangtze River as far as Hangkow.

By now, events around the world were beginning to escalate. While he was in China, Japan began bombing parts of China. During this conflict, the USS *Panay* was accidentally sunk causing a diplomatic stir in Shanghai. Meanwhile, Germany was posturing in Europe. The stage was being set.

In 1937, George carried out further Reserve training of several months as a Sub Lieutenant in HMS *Sheffield*, a cruiser. At the end of the year, the Captain, Mark Wardlaw, sent for George, looked seriously at him and said, 'I have no doubt whatever. You realise there is a war coming.'

'Yes Sir.'

'In the coming war, as a Royal Naval Reserve officer, you'll be called up, so whether you like it or not, you will be fighting in the war. You can continue the war in the Reserve, if you want to. However, the Admiralty is looking for officers such as yourself who can be transferred permanently right away into the Royal Navy. What do you think about that? Would you like to transfer?'

George didn't hesitate. 'Yes Sir, I will transfer.'

So, at the age of 21, at the end of that year and after an interview with the Admiralty in London, George was informed that he had been accepted as a permanent officer in the Royal Navy; it was noted that he had volunteered for submarines. In fact, the Admiralty finally selected 150 officers from the Reserve.

Another event at the end of that year stimulated George into action – Phoebe graduated as a physiotherapist. As she intended to return to Kimberley to work, George decided he should propose to her. When he asked what she would like for an engagement ring she replied, 'A Kimberley stone' (i.e. a diamond).

It was at this point that George decided to ask permission from Phoebe's father and 'do the right thing'. By coincidence, Joe Abrahams was returning to Kimberley briefly to see his family, so George asked Joe if he would deliver a letter to Phoebe's father in which George formally asked his permission to marry their daughter.

At this, Phoebe's mother immediately 'hot-footed' over from South Africa to Scotland to assess for herself what sort of family her daughter was marrying into. Luckily, she was captivated by George's loving and wonderful aunts and gave George her blessing. Joe, of course, had put in a good word for George, which helped.

So the pair journeyed to London and consulted with a friend, Wilfred Topp, who was the De Beers representative and who knew Phoebe's family. From here they selected a diamond and asked a jeweller to design a ring. Phoebe then went back with her mother to Kimberley, complete with her engagement ring and a promise, and began work in the Kimberley Hospital.

George transferred to the Royal Navy in February 1938 and spent that year on technical courses in gunnery, navigation, signals and torpedoes. During the year, he attended a junior officers' war course at Greenwich, where one of the strategies for 'getting to know your enemy' was to read *Mein Kampf*, a book written by Hitler and published in 1925–6. It combined elements of autobiography with an exposition of Hitler's National Socialist political ideology. It was disturbing and enlightening reading as the narrative described the process by which he became increasingly anti-Semitic, anti-communist and militaristic.

After a brief time in HMS *Foxhound*, a destroyer, George was accepted for and started training in submarines. Captain Cantlie's influence had been pivotal in his decision-making. He looked forward to the challenges.

On 1 January 1939, George began his training to qualify in submarines at HMS *Dolphin* near Portsmouth. *Dolphin* was known as a 'stone frigate' – it was a very old fort and was steeped in tradition and history. Directly across the harbour, Nelson once embarked from there, the 'Sally Port'.

Thirteen officers began the course. During their time as midshipmen, they had all been to sea in submarines, influencing their decision to volunteer for this arm of the naval service. Most of the time was spent in classrooms, but the men went to sea regularly for a day or two in an L-class submarine, either L26 or L27, the two submarines specifically allocated to the training class. These were medium-sized vessels and could stay at sea for about a month.

Even though George had been inside a submarine before (Captain Cantlie had seen to that), he was still intrigued to notice the degree of stability once inside the vessel after it had dived. When in the control room, the only awareness that the boat was submerging was a slight motion of the bows going down and later a gentle levelling off. No notion of panic or claustrophobia.

In addition to learning about the complicated working of a submarine, the class was also indoctrinated in all the skills on how to escape from a sunken submarine. They particularly learned about the physiological side of escape gear, pressure, equipment and associated problems.

Unfortunately, during that year George received some sad news. His father retired from Uganda and on the very day he arrived back in Scotland, he died. It distressed George considerably as he had not seen his parents in thirteen years. Even though his relationship with his father had been somewhat distant, George had now become fully aware of the sacrifice made by his parents towards his wellbeing and future. This included making all the necessary arrangements, at a very considerable financial outlay, to ensure that he received an excellent education in Scotland. They had, of course, been confident he would be well looked after by his father's two sisters, who became dearly loved by George.

After burying his father, and without seeing George (who was at sea), his mother immediately returned to East Africa to work in the hospital at Nairobi in Kenya. There, she became a 'Sister Tutor', teaching Kenyan nurses, as she was fluent in Swahili. George wondered when he would see her again.

But George's life was about to change in a big way when, in April 1939, he took up his first appointment in a submarine, HMS *Unity*.

CHAPTER TWO

The Opening Shots

By early 1939, the Admiralty were well aware of the potential for war and issued new war plans. These allowed for war against Germany and Italy simultaneously, with France as an ally, while recognizing that Japan was unfriendly and that it was necessary to keep a defensive posture against her in the Far East.

By a superhuman effort in all departments, the Reserve Fleet was brought out of their 'care and maintenance' sojourn (mothballs). By July, the ships had been manned, stored, fuelled and armed. Those responsible were so efficient that, after a quick review by the King, the Reserve Fleet was declared 'in all aspects ready for war'. It was then absorbed into the rest of the Navy which was in the process of being dispersed to war stations. The Royal Navy was ready.

The plan for submarines provided for reinforcement of the Mediterranean with six submarines, and for fifteen to remain in the Far East. All other submarines (twenty-one of them) would be concentrated in the North Sea as part of the Home Fleet.

HMS *Unity* formed part of one of these North Sea flotillas with their operational role being to form outposts for reconnaissance off the exits of the German bases in the Heligoland Bight and in the Skagerrak. Their main task was to give warning should units of the German Fleet, especially the pocket battleships, attempt to break out into the trade routes. *Unity*'s home port was at Blyth, on the east coast of England, a submarine base that had also been used in the First World War.

Unity's first patrol, with George on board, sailed on 2 August 1939, to keep watch off Heligoland, at the mouth of the River Elbe. The patrol was largely uneventful and *Unity* was recalled after two weeks. She left again for the same area on 22 August, which is where George was on 3 September, when *Unity* received a signal that war had at last been declared. For a submarine to receive a message while underwater, it requires a very low radio frequency (VLF) of about 16 kilocycles. Communication was achieved using Morse codes or cyphers, via a special loop aerial. These were transmitted from the naval wireless station in Rugby, central England. However, while underwater, submarines could only receive radio messages, not send them. Radio messages could only be transmitted while the submarine was on the surface, by raising a telescopic or a hinged mast. (The little H-Class submarine would fly a kite which carried the aerial well up. However, it was very seldom used, for obvious reasons.)

The other important transmitting device was the Asdic. The Asdic transducer was, first and foremost, a hydrophone, simply for listening to the noise made by propellers. However, it could also transmit under water and in this active mode it was a range-finding device. It could detect mines in certain cases, or a submerged submarine thereby revealing its position. When just listening, it was sensitive enough to detect noisy pumps of an enemy vessel or a hammer strike during repairs. It could also be used for communication between submerged submarines.

For a submarine, secrecy during the war was of the utmost importance. It was imperative that the enemy had no idea of its presence. If any mechanisms were transmitting, such as sending a radio signal, using the radar or Asdic 'pinging', and were detected, it could very quickly give the game away.

Asdic took its name from the initials of the Anglo-French committee which invented it – the Allied Submarine Detection Investigation Committee. It consisted of a transmitter/receiver encased in a metal dome which was housed forward; on a surface vessel, it was usually under the keel of the ship. It comprised quartz crystals which would fluctuate on an electrical impulse which could send out sound emissions on any selected bearing. When the sound waves struck an object, they were reflected and picked up. The device was associated with a characteristic 'ping', a sound which became frighteningly familiar to all submariners.

As *Unity* had been to Heligoland twice in the previous month, largely uneventfully, the announcement of war was greeted with a general feeling of relief. The sentiments were, 'Thank God, the buggers have made a decision. Now we can get on with this war and get it over with.'

However, there was some indignation that first day as a German U-boat, *U30*, sank a large passenger ship, the *Athenia*, in mid-Atlantic. The *Athenia* was full of British women and children who were being evacuated to the safety of Canada. The Germans were ignoring international law and it was obvious Hitler was going to fight under a different set of rules.

At this stage of the war, the Royal Navy was fighting under what was called the Prize Manual Regulations, which had also been signed by Germany. These rules were developed in the days of buccaneering, when a British ship could bring in an 'enemy' ship as a 'prize' and be paid for it – as 'prize money'. The rules insisted that an attack on merchant vessels had to be in accordance with these regulations, which involved 'visit and search'. Merchant ships could not be sunk without provision being made for the safety of the crew and passengers, although naval ships could be sunk without warning. This condition was not considered to be met by leaving the crew and passengers of merchant ships at sea in the ship's boats.

This confining rule basically meant the submarine had to surface, confront the enemy ship or fire a shot across its bow, and then supervise civilians into a situation where they could be rescued. In those early days, the problem was that it was not easy to determine a Merchant Navy ship from a naval ship. Worse, merchant vessels were often escorted by a destroyer or corvette, so to expose yourself in this situation would have been akin to suicide. Also, some merchant vessels had been armed with one or more guns, plus the gunners to man them. Eventually, the Admiralty realized they were fighting the war with one hand tied behind their back. By March 1940, they established 'Sink on sight' rules for all enemy ships.

In the meantime, in Kimberley, as soon as war was declared, Phoebe, who was working in a South African hospital, declared, 'Right. I'm coming over.' In October, along with some nurses, medical personnel and other Britons trying to return to Britain, Phoebe sailed by the Union Castle Shipping Line. It was a dangerous crossing as the convoy was unescorted and the ship zigzagged most of the way.

Phoebe went straight to Edinburgh where George's two aunts greeted her. The plan was to marry George on 24 November at Edinburgh. The aunts, both of whom had lost their intendeds in the First World War, warmed to this job, and organized the church and virtually the whole wedding – which almost didn't go to plan.

George had been on patrol in the *Unity* and, while returning, received a signal that the Germans had laid mines around the Firth of Forth, the entrance to Rosyth near Edinburgh. This meant that the *Unity* was diverted to Blyth. Eventually he arrived in Edinburgh the day before the wedding, but with no decent uniform or clothes. The original plan called for his clothes to be sent by rail from Blyth, some two hours south, but the clothes were detained somewhere in the railway system.

A little forlornly, and with a touch of irony and humour, he commented, 'I have nothing to wear.' Then, with a strong sense of purpose, he bought a suitcase at one end of Princes Street in Edinburgh and walked the length of the street until he had bought a new set of clothes. He was particularly grateful when he entered Gieves, the naval tailor (they outfitted Nelson), and explained the situation. Luckily, he had been known there since he had been a cadet. Mr Logie, the manager, welcomed him and rose to the challenge; he was soon fitted out in full with a new uniform. The wedding did go to plan, with Joe Abrahams acting as George's best man. The event was recorded by a Kodak expert who captured the moment on an 8mm film, copies of which were sent to Phoebe's mother in South Africa and George's mother in Uganda.

The newlyweds were able to fit in a two-day honeymoon in London. All too briefly, it was over and they caught a train back to Blyth, where they were able to live together while George continued his work. Occasionally, when George knew he was to go on a long patrol, Phoebe would stay with the aunts in Scotland.

This is what the plan was for the fateful seventh patrol on 29 April 1940. Just before George left at 4.00pm that day, Phoebe said, 'Tomorrow morning, I'll get the 10.00am train back to Scotland. See you when you get back.'

George said goodbye and walked down to the docks to meet the new captain of the *Unity*. They then left to patrol the seas off Heligoland.

CHAPTER THREE

HMS *Unity*

The *Unity* never reached Heligoland.

As described in the Prologue, the *Unity* was involved in a collision with the Norwegian vessel *Alte Jarl*. We left George and the *Unity* spiralling into the cold waters of the North Sea, off the coast of England...

* * *

The submarine HMS *Unity* smashed into the sea bed in about 100 feet of water. George, tumbling helplessly in its wake, was now struggling at about 90 feet. He felt, rather than heard, the muffled thud of the submarine as it thumped into the muddy rock and sand below him. He was in some distress as the pain in his ears had been building and the pressure was now at about 45lb a square inch (three times the pressure at ground level, 14.7lb per square inch).

Then, suddenly, the relentless down-pull of the suction eased. George felt a tremendous release as he became liberated from the potency of its grip. He was now out of the pull of the rampaging vessel and desperately kicked upwards. He searched for the surface and swam strongly towards it.

Internally, he had remained reasonably calm, was aware it would take him about ten seconds to reach the surface. His training had taught him that a fit person can, given the buoyancy of a proper life-jacket (which of course, no one had), propel himself upwards at 6 feet a second. He simply needed to hang on. Finally, with lungs bursting, he splashed through to the surface and gasped for life-giving oxygen.

Within a few seconds his breathing settled and his mind cleared. He quickly assessed his situation. Apart from a very painful arm, which he couldn't remember damaging, and pain in both ears, he became satisfied he was basically alright. During the drama of surfacing, he had been distracted temporarily from his ear problems and noticed other men who had splashed to the surface were trying to organize themselves. He made contact with Lieutenant Trickey and his Captain, who had also been dragged deep below and now bounced to the surface. Trickey seemed to be alright, but the Captain was nursing a very sore head which had smacked into something during his ordeal. He spluttered and, in between trying to blow more air into his lifebelt, said: 'Well, now we know at first hand what it is like to be "sucked down" and I don't ever want to do that again! I always thought it was a bit of a myth that you'd be dragged down after the ship!'

The three officers swam around to the thirty-odd men and tried to keep them together. Even though the rubber life-saving ring (or belt) helped to keep them reasonably buoyant, it was fairly inefficient in the swell and the sailors had to tread water vigorously. It was tiring work and the water was cold, sapping energy. The men were also caught in a sluicing (fast-flowing) tide. Some men started singing to maintain their spirits, but George called to them, 'Better save your breath for staying afloat.'

There was no way of them knowing how long they might be here as there had been no chance to send an SOS and they would not be expected home for about a fortnight. This was a potentially serious situation.

Men were tiring fast. George noticed that two of them in particular appeared to be having grave difficulties. They began drifting off in the darkness and swirling mists, the sea clawing at them. Then, after about forty-five minutes, George heard the sweet sound of a ship coming towards them. In a few seconds, the *Alte Jarl* broke out of the fog. To his relief, the Norwegian ship had returned and found them. A searchlight raced over the water and highlighted the struggling men. They were saved. Two boats were quickly launched and moved among the submariners, picking up each of the men in turn.

31

Once on board, the crew were well looked after and taken down to the engine room where they could dry out. After dressing in borrowed dry clothes, the Captain and George went up to the bridge and talked to the Norwegian Captain and Chief Officer.

By now, George realised they had lost four men: Angus Low and Henry Miller, who were caught inside the bowels of the submarine, and the two sailors who were last seen disappearing into the dark.

The Captain of the *Alte Jarl* said they were part of a large convoy going south. He said that once he realized he had rammed a British submarine, by the time he had turned around, they had the difficulty of avoiding the other ships in the convoy, otherwise they would have come to the rescue earlier.

The Norwegian ship, in common with many merchant ships, wasn't compelled to have a radio in those days, so the British sailors could not immediately report to their base. As the *Alte Jarl* was part of a large convoy of merchant ships, the Captain tried to find and get close to another ship to relay a message, but it was not going to be easy, or even safe, in the fog. From every direction, echoing out of the darkness, the Captain was warned by the ringing of multiple bells. (When a ship is hidden in fog, ringing a bell indicates that she is at anchor.) Eventually, in his wisdom, the Captain decided that negotiating by sound was too dangerous and he opted to anchor his ship for the night also, an action for which George was grateful.

In the morning, at first light, as the mist cleared, George noticed a British destroyer sitting at anchor in the middle of the great number of merchant ships. He admired the ability of the *Alte Jarl*'s Captain to manoeuvre his way into the middle of this group without incident. The Captain then authorized a signalman to flash a message to the destroyer, by shining an Aldis light, an instrument which emits a light beam towards its target. The signal, emitted in Morse, said: 'Please pass to HMS *Elfin*,' (*Unity*'s base). 'Regret to report HMS *Unity* sunk.'

The destroyer then relayed the message on to Blyth, the home base. At 6.00am, the crew of the *Unity* were landed at North Shields, a town just south of Blyth at the mouth of the Tyne River.

The British sailors were a ragged-looking bunch and the rumour had obviously been passed out to the local population that they were

German U-boat prisoners. The locals responded with resounding boos, heckling and some anger. The sailors, in turn, replied with a tirade of colourful English expletives, leaving no doubt as to their British nationality. The rejoinder had its effect. Immediately, the harassment turned to hearty cheers!

Meanwhile, a bus had been sent from Blyth which the men boarded. It was only a short journey back to the town and by 8.00am they were home. George went straight to his digs, where Phoebe met him at the front door and welcomed him home. She had not received the message relating to *Unity*'s misadventure and amazingly did not notice George was out of uniform, that he was wearing borrowed clothes and was barefoot. She said unconcernedly, 'Oh, you didn't go after all. That's lovely. I won't have to go up to the aunts.'

Luckily she hadn't had time to be upset at his news or even immediately understand the gravity of George's recent predicament. Instead, she was distressed for Angus Low's wife, Marjorie. She had become a close friend of Marjorie's, who was a cypher officer in the Wrens (the title given to women in the WRNS – Women's Royal Naval Service). When Phoebe joined the base, she didn't work as a physiotherapist but instead joined the Wrens, as had the wives of many of the other sailors, boosting the manpower. Unlike Marjorie, she was a Regulating Chief Petty Officer. All the women understood the risks involved and would rally to support each other in time of crisis and loss. Phoebe immediately went around to comfort Marjorie.

The following day George was called to attend the Court of Enquiry, a process where all parties concerned are interviewed when a ship is lost at sea. After listening to all the witnesses, the court found that there were various procedures which could have been done better. There had been a breakdown in communication in that *Unity* had not been made aware of the approaching convoy. There was also a rising awareness that submarines in British waters should be accompanied by an escort. In the end, the court found that there had been 'a collision' and there was insufficient evidence to attach blame solely to any one person. The case was closed.

What was certain was very clear. Submarines were very involved in this war. HMS *Unity* was the eighth Royal Naval submarine to be sunk in the first eight months of the war.

This now allowed George to take advantage of seven days survivor's leave, providing an excellent chance to catch up on his recent short honeymoon. His plan was to spend time with Phoebe at Loch Lomond. A cousin of his had a sailing dinghy there and said he was welcome to use it. It sounded ideal. However, the best laid plans . . .

The next day George and Phoebe travelled to Scotland to stay at the Luss Hotel on the loch. George had just finished unpacking his clothes when a policeman arrived and knocked at his door.

'Are you Lieutenant Hunt?' he asked.

'Yes, I am.'

'I have a telegram for you.'

George opened the telegram. The message was blunt. It said simply: 'Report to HMS *Dolphin* forthwith.'

So much for his survivor's leave!

CHAPTER FOUR

HMS *Proteus*

George immediately travelled to Portsmouth. He knew HMS *Dolphin* well having completed his basic submarine training there, and went directly to the staff office.

'You sent for me, Sir?'

'Yes Hunt. Sorry about *Unity* and your leave. You may well know that Germany has now occupied Holland. As such, Queen Wilhelmina and the Dutch cabinet have all been spirited away to England. Some of the Dutch Fleet and most of their submarines have also whisked over here to join us. One of them, *O10*, is lying down there in the trot. You will be her Liaison Officer. You will take with you a Petty Officer Telegraphist and a signalman, and I will set you up with code and cypher books.'

The Dutch submarine *O10* was the same size as the British U-class subs, and George joined with his two specialists. He immediately enjoyed the Dutchmen's company and familiarized himself with the workings of the submarine.

At this stage, all the eyes of the world were on France as Hitler was ruthlessly but brilliantly pursuing his blitzkrieg tactics (lightning strike) and was herding the British Expeditionary Force (BEF) onto the beaches of Dunkirk.

As early as 20 May 1940, the Navy had started planning what it called Operation DYNAMO. No one knew how many of the men in the BEF would reach Dunkirk, but it was obvious that rescuing them would require every vessel that could be found.

The Dutchmen in *O10* were only too willing to help – they had an axe to grind. The armada that set forth on 26 May presented an unbelievable sight. Pouring out from many English ports, including Portsmouth, was a fleet whose infinite variety had never been seen before. Alongside destroyers were personnel ships, fishing trawlers, fireboats, paddle-wheelers, barges and private launches. All were endeavouring to rescue the stranded fighting men in France – probably as many as 300,000 – and were prepared to run the gauntlet of Stuka dive-bombers.

One worry to George and the crew of *O10* was that the English Channel had been heavily mined, but the Royal Navy had swept three narrow channels across to the Continent. The job of *O10* was to give early warning of any approaching enemy surface ships. As they patrolled the channels, protecting the vast, motley fleet while it spirited the remnants of the British and Allied Forces back to England, the submariners were tense but fascinated. The largest concern was the German dive-bombers which created havoc all around. Any ship in their sights was virtually a sitting duck. To George's great relief, the *O10* wasn't targeted. The evacuation lasted until 1 June. At the end of this 'longest day', they joined in the elation knowing that they were part of one of the greatest feats in military history. Many men were saved; most would eventually be retrained and would fight another day.

George did one more patrol with the *O10* and then, in August 1940, he was appointed First Lieutenant and Second-in-Command of HM Submarine *H31*. The *H31* was a simple and very attractive old submarine which had been built in Canada during the First World War.

Initially, their role wasn't particularly rewarding, with the submarine being used to carry out anti-submarine training for Allied destroyers. *H31* acted mostly as a 'clockwork mouse' for the Asdic operators who were hidden away in the cabin of the destroyers, trying to locate and 'ping' off the sub. The submarine would tow several round red spheres called 'buffs' which would float on the surface behind them. In this way, the Captain on the bridge of the destroyer could visibly track the submarine's position, and then relate it to how his Asdic team was performing.

H31 then undertook two tough patrols in the Bay of Biscay off the north-west coast of France. The Germans had developed two strong U-boat bases in this area at Brest and Lorient, from where German submarines would leave to attack Allied convoys carrying supplies from North America to England via the Atlantic.

It was a most inhospitable place to lie in wait. The north-west coast was rocky and unforgiving, and the great Atlantic rollers crashed above and around them. Most of the time, the seas were so rough they had to patrol on the surface and search for enemy ships through binoculars. The conditions were miserable, often intolerable. As well as being bitterly cold, large rogue waves regularly swamped the conning tower, dousing everybody on the bridge. For their trouble, they didn't sight one enemy ship or submarine.

In November, 1940, George was ordered to report to the large shipbuilding firm of Vickers Armstrong at Barrow in Furness on the north-west coast of England. He was to 'stand by' the building of a new Unity-class submarine, the *Urchin*, in which he was to be the First Lieutenant. However, he was told, 'We're going to give the *Urchin* to the Polish Navy. Like the Dutch, some of the Poles have been able to get away from the German occupation and are itching to hit back. You will be the Liaison Officer. As you've been with U-class submarines for so long, we want you to be with them for the remainder of the building period, then the trials and work-up. Then you will go off to the Mediterranean as First Lieutenant of *Proteus*.'

The Polish Captain was Lieutenant Commander Boris Karnicki. He and all the Polish sailors were very efficient and charming, the ladies finding them particularly captivating. On being introduced, they would click their heels, bow and kiss the woman's hand.

At this stage, Phoebe had the rank of Chief Petty Officer in the Women's RN Service and was in charge of about 150 Wrens. She was given a short leave to go to Vickers with George and soon befriended some of the wives of the Polish sailors. Even though George could speak no Polish, the Poles could speak excellent English, particularly the officers. They therefore got on very well. The entourage travelled by train to London, then continued north to Barrow in Furness. When they arrived at Vickers, the Managing

Director, Sir Charles Craven, a former submariner, ensured they had good accommodation and were well looked after.

This was a very busy period covering, as it did, all the torpedo and noise trials, as well as diving trials, inspections and final acceptance of the submarine from the builders. However, George found the Poles to be very professional and keen.

The majority of these trials were conducted in the Firth of Clyde and its many lochs. There were some periods of relaxation during which George taught the Poles some basic Scottish country dancing, an activity the Poles really seemed to enjoy – to the extent that when the local lads and lassies invited the Poles to dances, George was delighted to see that Boris Karnicki and his merry men acquitted themselves well, to the applause of their hosts. In return, the Poles taught George and some friends a highly dangerous Polish dance involving the brandishing of real axes in a fearsome manner. It wasn't all hard work and no play.

While here, George received the good news that he had been awarded a Mention in Dispatches (MiD) in the 1941 New Year's Honours List. This was for his bravery and leadership during the *Unity* sinking. He was pleased to hear that Angus Low and Henry Miller both received posthumous George Crosses. Celebrations were enjoyed all around.

At a ceremony attended by Admiral Sir Max Horton, Flag Officer Submarines, and General Sikorski, the Senior Polish Officer in Britain, the *Urchin* was renamed the ORP *Sokol* (the Polish word for falcon). George worked with the Poles for five months and found it was an enjoyable and rewarding association in many ways, although he wasn't seeing much action. But that was about to change.

In April 1941, George was appointed First Lieutenant of HMS *Proteus* which was one of the O, P and R classes and one of the larger patrol submarines. She had been built and engineered also by Vickers Armstrong and was launched in July 1929. When the war broke out, she was at Singapore as a unit of the Fourth Submarine Flotilla, and was transferred in May 1940 to join the First Flotilla at Alexandria in Egypt. She had just returned from a tour of duty in the Mediterranean and was now in dry dock at Portsmouth, undergoing repairs. George joined her there.

The *Proteus* was designed for endurance and had well-planned accommodation quarters. This allowed some comfort for her crew of fifty, but she was also well constructed for war. She had a powerful torpedo armament of six bow tubes with six reloads, plus two stern tubes aft and two reloads. She was also equipped with an effective and powerful 4-inch gun set in a rotating breastwork just forward of the conning tower. The gun had its own quick-manning hatches to allow independent access from inside the submarine.

At this stage in the war, Portsmouth was being bombed. During one attack George noticed some incendiary bombs had fallen onto the casing of the submarine. To his dismay, he also witnessed one of the workers on the hull kick several of the burning incendiaries onto the floor of the dock. As the blocks supporting the submarine were made of wood, George quickly organized a party to go to the bottom of the docks and extinguish the bombs.

The Captain, Lieutenant Commander Phillip Francis, was, before the war, an adventurer and a very experienced sailor, having already had a book written about his sailing exploits. As Second-in-Command, George knew he could learn a great deal from him. As such, he was full of high expectations as the *Proteus* began her return journey to the Mediterranean in July 1941.

George took his own role very seriously. He was directly responsible to the Captain and was virtually in charge of the maintenance and running of the boat. His job was to oversee the needs and wellbeing of the fifty crewmen, their examinations, their behaviour and standards, and their punishments. He was also responsible for the cleanliness of the boat and was the co-ordinator of all the systems that make a boat work.

Further responsibilities included supervision that gun drill was carried out and that torpedo loading and firing arrangements all worked. In this regard, he worked in close co-ordination with the Gunnery Officer, Jeremy Nash. Nash was a splendid Dartmouth-trained officer, cheerful and efficient. (He subsequently took over as First Lieutenant when George left the *Proteus*.) The Navigation Officer was Con Thode, a New Zealander, who was a keen yachtsman and an officer of the RNZNVR. The Engineer Officer was Peter Scott-Maxwell. His job was to oversee the engines and all mechanical aspects of the boat. Maxwell was an old friend whom George had known in Glasgow before the war and who was very much a 'hands-on' engineer, just right for a submarine.

What was most interesting to George was that the *Proteus* was the first British submarine to be fitted with radar. It was actually the same design as used by the Royal Air Force except that the aerial had been 'marinized', as they put it. This required the aerial equipment to be able to withstand the pressure created by deep diving. The apparatus was very primitive and because the study of radar was brand new, *Proteus* had two Dundee university students manning the set. Their names were Dot and Bendle.

Dot and Bendle protected their territory with some zeal and a little humour. The radar was creating some interest among the crew and was viewed with a modicum of mystery. The Chief Engine Room Artificer, who was 'Lord of all he surveyed' in the engine room, tentatively poked his head into the radar room. Bendle said, 'I wouldna' stand there if I were you Chief, it will render you sterile.' Not prepared to debate or test the point, the Chief removed himself quickly.

Proteus' first call was to the British territory of Gibraltar where they refuelled and picked up supplies for the defence of Malta. Normally in a submarine, the saddle tanks are flooded with sea water for diving. Some of these were closed off and refilled with aviation fuel which was to be transferred to Malta.

Since September 1940, Malta had been under siege. By reason of its geography and its British heritage, the island was proving a nasty thorn for the Germans. It sat right in the centre of the Mediterranean. For the Germans to reinforce Rommel's Afrika Korps fighting in Libya, their supply ships, which set out from Italy, had to run the gauntlet past Malta. The enemy were paying a heavy price for Italy's lack of foresight in not capturing Malta before commencing their campaign to conquer Egypt.

Proteus quietly slipped into Malta and delivered the fuel and stores to the dockyard, then continued on to her final destination and base at Alexandria in Egypt.

At this stage of the war, the Desert Campaign in Egypt and Libya was in full swing. Rommel, the audacious and brilliant German general who had earlier in May 1940 raced his 7th Panzer (tank) Division across France, helping to press the Allied army onto the beaches of Dunkirk, was now pushing the British Eighth Army out of Libya towards Egypt.

By 11 April 1941, Easter, the 9th Australian Division swelled the ranks of other British and Commonwealth units established in Tobruk in Libya. Rommel, who was intent on conquering Egypt and the Suez Canal, found himself halted on the threshold of triumph by this single impudent Allied garrison. He could not push beyond it without first taking it.

By the time the *Proteus* had reached the Mediterranean, Tobruk had been under siege for some six months. Her 'mother' (depot) ship at Alexandria was *Medway*, having earlier been transferred from Singapore. (At this stage, the Japanese threat in the Pacific was not perceived as large.) The depot ship was a veritable floating city. She had sufficient mess decks, workshops, stores, torpedoes and provisions to care for a submarine squadron. Now she had twelve submarines in her care. As well as being the supply ship, *Medway* had at her disposal a full spare submarine crew on standby – from a captain of a submarine to an able seaman. If somebody became injured or ill, there was an immediate replacement. There was also a Greek 'mother' ship docked at Alexandria, the *Corinthian*, with four submarines.

The nucleus of another flotilla, the Eighth, had been formed at Gibraltar with *Maidstone* as its depot ship. In addition, a naval captain had arrived in Malta in January to set up the Tenth Flotilla. The priority of these submarines was to harass the enemy along the coast of Italy and North Africa, basically to prevent supplies getting through to Rommel.

However, George's first patrol in the Middle East was to the Aegean Sea and it was largely unsuccessful. On 28 September, the *Proteus* left to monitor the seas off Zante (Zakynthos) Island in Greece. After two abortive attacks, her telemotor system malfunctioned and she returned to Alexandria on 12 October for alterations and repairs.

George's next patrol, however, was more productive. On 26 October, the *Proteus* left for a patrol in the Gulf of Athens (Saronic Gulf). Having reconnoitred Candia (Iraklio) and Suda Bay on the north coast of Crete, they took up a waiting position south-west of the Doro Channel. On the night of 3/4 November, they were lying on the surface recharging their batteries.

Submarines have large banks of batteries which power the boat while submerged. Each battery contained 112 cells and each cell weighed a half ton, requiring regular maintenance. The diesel engines, acting as generators, recharged these batteries at night under cover of darkness while on the surface, a function which often might take three to six hours, depending on the state of the battery.

This night, while George was in the control room, the radar screen came to life. He was intrigued. The receiving monitor, about 20x25cm in size, consisted of a dark screen with a rudimentary base line crackling across it. The base line, to George, looked like a row of green grass. When the radar beam reflected a signal off an object, 'green grass leaves' would shoot up, creating a 'blip'. Dot and Bendle, the operators, reported, 'Contact. Bearing red 85°.' They thought there might well be a convoy of two or three ships out there.

It could only be the enemy.

The Captain decided to trust the new gadgetry and opted to shadow the ships while the submarine was still recharging. The submarine possessed two large diesel engines and it was possible to recharge with one engine while propelling the vessel with the other. *Proteus* followed the 'blips' all night by radar at a safe distance. By now, they were just east of Andros Island in the Aegean. Then just before sunrise, as they crept closer, they could hear the engines of the enemy ships. The Captain laid out his plans.

'We'll go to diving stations now. I intend to get ahead of them and wait for them to approach. The aim is to get to a position so that they will go across the path of the rising sun, then we'll attack.'

The target ship was the Italian tanker *Tampico* which was fully laden and, at 4,958 tons, was too good a prize to miss. However, she was escorted by two destroyers, *Monzambano* and *Castelfidardo*. *Proteus* dived and waited about 900m (1,000 yards) ahead of

Tampico, but had some concerns as one destroyer passed close to *Proteus'* stern.

Captain Francis maintained his resolve and fired three torpedoes at the tanker. As the torpedoes raced towards their prey, George waited for the sound of a muffled explosion. He was rewarded as one of the torpedoes struck the *Tampico*, which immediately began to take in water. Realizing the escorts would quickly retaliate, the *Proteus* dived to about 200 feet (61m) and waited. The Captain ordered, 'Shut off for depth charging and silent routine.'

(Depth charges had been introduced during the latter part of the First World War and were similar in shape to a 40-gallon drum. They contained 300lb (163.37kg) of amatol explosive. They were normally dropped from rails over the stern and fired over both quarters by mechanical throwers. On entering the water, the depth charge sank at about 10 feet per second and could be set to detonate at varying depths. For it to be really effective, the attacking vessel had to be virtually over the submarine.)

The Asdic operators quickly took off their headphones – an exploding depth charge in the vicinity could permanently damage eardrums. Within a few minutes, the sound of erupting depth charges reverberated through the boat. Strong shock waves vibrated and the boat shuddered. Everything that wasn't secure rattled; some crockery fell and smashed. To George's interest, everyone, including himself, remained calm and quiet, and methodically went about their business. The counter-attack was accurate and dangerously close, but in reality inflicted little damage on *Proteus*.

After some time, the battering from the depth charges diminished and the escorts moved further away. Eventually, the *Proteus* rose to periscope depth some distance from the enemy ships. The Captain noticed that the *Tampico* was listing heavily and was sitting very low in the water. He had not meted out enough damage to sink her quickly but he need not try again. That would be enough.

Proteus moved away from the region and for the next few days patrolled the area around St Giorgios Island. On the night of 9/10 November, again while on the surface, her radar picked up another convoy. This time, the Captain decided to be more adventurous – he would shadow the ships and wait for the rising of the moon. He would then attack if there was enough light.

Proteus patiently shadowed the main ship of the convoy, the 1,773-ton *Ithaka*, for six hours. (The *Ithaka* was now a German ship, formerly Greek.) Eventually the rising moon bathed the sea, and the *Ithaka*, with a brilliant silver sheen. The radiance allowed clear visual sighting. The *Proteus* submerged and then stealthily approached to within 600 yards (550m) of the *Ithaka*. They were now just a few kilometres south-west of the Greek island of Milos. The Captain ordered four torpedoes to be fired, two of which smashed into the ship and she very quickly sank.

Proteus returned to Alexandria on the 15th after a most successful patrol. It was the first time that radar was used in action by a British submarine and had also been a notable use of the moon to make a submerged attack at night.

On the larger scene, Allied submarines were steadily making a considerable impact on the balance of power in the Mediterranean. By November, Germany had sent twenty U-boats to help redress the losses incurred by aggressive Allied submarine attacks. The total successes in the whole of the Mediterranean by Allied submarines during November were a destroyer, a cruiser and five large merchant vessels. There had been no losses of British or Allied submarines from any of the three flotillas (Gibraltar, Malta and Alexandria) during the month.

Their total strength stood at twenty-three British, two Netherlands, one Polish (the *Sokol*, based at Malta – George knew her well, having served originally as the Liaison Officer) and five Greek submarines.

On 28 November 1941, the *Proteus* left for a patrol in the Kithera Channel in the Aegean Sea. The Germans had a strong presence on the Greek Islands. By the end of May 1941, Crete and most of the Greek Islands were in German hands. As such, they had commandeered many of the local inter-island ferry boats called caiques. These were traditional Greek wooden cargo sailing ships and varied in size from 40 to 700 tons. They had a distinctive pointed bow and high stern, a broad beam and were fitted with various sail plans. The enemy would use these vessels to transport supplies and troops to Crete and around the Greek Islands – indeed they were entirely dependent on seizing and using the caiques.

Through the periscope, Captain Francis could see one of these caiques, with five German soldiers on board. In order to save firing a precious torpedo, he edged *Proteus* right up to the ship and suddenly surfaced alongside. Then, while the surprised and frustrated soldiers were kept at bay by the Gunnery Officer directing the boat's weapon at them, two explosive experts boarded the caique. They placed dynamite plugs in the hold of the ship and proceeded to blow holes in the bottom of it – a cheap and effective method of destroying a vessel.

December brought changes to the balance of world power. On 7 December, while George and the *Proteus* were on patrol, the United States and Japan entered the conflict, significantly altering the dynamics. Even though the news that Japanese torpedo-bombers had attacked Pearl Harbor was both disturbing, and to most, enlightening, the effect wasn't immediately relevant to those in the Mediterranean. However, there was quiet relief that the United States would now enter the war.

Much more concerning was the news that the two great British battleships, *Prince of Wales* and *Repulse*, had been sunk off Malaya on the 10th. They had been sent there to monitor the aggressive Japanese expansion and be ready to defend Singapore.

In the meantime, in the Mediterranean, the pressure was still full on for the men in *Proteus*. On 22 December, she carried out a patrol off the Greek island of Cephalonia. On the 30th, she intercepted the 2,480-ton *Citta di Marsala*. The conditions were flat calm but the attack was hampered by the presence of both air and sea escorts. The torpedoes seriously damaged her, but the *Proteus* could not get close enough to deliver a *coup de grâce*. There was some satisfaction in finding out later that she was towed back to the east coast of Sicily and beached.

On 5 January 1942, while off Cape Dukato in Levkas, Greece, *Proteus* intercepted the *Citta di Palermo*, a large transport ship of 5,413 tons. The two torpedoes which were fired from the stern happened to be 21-inch Mark IIs. Torpedoes were expensive and very accountable, each torpedo being meticulously maintained with its own history sheet. During peacetime, they were often fired, recovered and reused. George was amazed to find these two were built in 1916, the year he was born. He discovered that these particular Mark IIs had originally been part of an R-class battleship armament in the First World War. Their long duty of care was rewarded as the *Citta di Palermo* immediately sank. *Proteus* returned to Alexandria on 12 January after a stormy passage home, finishing another successful patrol.

By late January 1942, George had taken part in five action-filled patrols. His time on board had been rewarding as he had been involved in the sinking of twelve enemy ships. His submarine-warfare experience was mounting, but a challenging incident while on his sixth patrol would test him much further.

The *Proteus* left Alexandria on 29 January for another patrol off Cephalonia, their mission being uneventful until 8 February. The incident occurred on the darkest of nights as the *Proteus* was, once again, cruising on the surface recharging her batteries. Conditions were generally miserable. The weather was squally, lashing the ocean with torrential downpours. Driving rain whipped across the front of the conning tower, further cutting visibility. The Captain and the OOW, who was Jeremy Nash, were on the bridge while George, as First Lieutenant, was in charge down below in the control room.

Through the inky matrix, the Captain caught sight of a dark shape looming some distance astern of the submarine. 'I think it's a U-boat,' he said to the OOW.

'Yes, Sir, I agree.'

There wasn't time to manoeuvre to fire his bow torpedoes. Instead, he fired the two stern torpedoes. At the same time, he ordered, 'Gun Action Stations!'

The words echoed down the voice pipe. Within seconds, the three-man gun crew had scrambled onto the wardroom table, crawled up and out of the hatch. As they assumed their positions behind the gun, the two torpedoes shot out from the rear tubes. Unfortunately, within a minute, the Captain realized they had missed their target, both torpedoes trailing harmlessly into the black sea.

The enemy ship responded by instantly turning towards the *Proteus*. Captain Francis and Nash noticed, to their horror, an ever-increasing bow wave, a large frothy, white wall, racing towards them. They realized this wave wasn't being created by a U-boat but by a destroyer and it was clearly intending to ram them.

The ship was, in fact, the Italian destroyer *Sagittario* which was approaching at such speed. It quickly became obvious to the Captain there was not going to be time for *Proteus* to dive to a safe depth. In that instant, the Captain decided that audacity was the best method of defence – he would counter by meeting the enemy absolutely head on.

He called down the voice pipe to the helmsman, giving him a series of orders to turn the submarine round to face the enemy. George, at this stage, was not fully aware of the drama being played out above. His main concern was that the amps were pouring out of the batteries and he was worried that if they dived now, they would not have enough power for a full day's dive ahead. He therefore leaned over to the voice pipe and called up to the Captain. He reminded him that they were still on the electric motors and not on the diesel engines. He said they were 'using up all the batteries'. George felt the Captain was using them unnecessarily but he resisted saying that to him. The Captain called back down the pipe, 'You wouldn't be worried about the bloody batteries if you were up here!'

'What's going on?' George asked.

'Collision Stations!' he called back. George didn't ask any more questions!

The voice pipe in the control room was also used by the Helmsman. Nash, the OOW, standing next to the Captain, called down to the Helmsman, 'Tell the First Lieutenant we're going to meet the destroyer absolutely head on.'

There was no need to say any more. The other men heard the statement and looked incredulously at each other.

The event happened so quickly there was no time for anyone to show any signs of fear. In fact, it was so fast neither the enemy ship

47

nor the *Proteus* gun crew on the fore deck had time to fire a shot! The gun crew watched hypnotically, enthralled as the destroyer narrowed the gap. To the men below there was no estimation of exactly where or when they would collide. They automatically focused on well-drilled emergency procedures.

For George, there was no chance to find out any more information from the Captain as the Captain called rapid commands to the helmsman, 'Port 15°, Midships, Starboard 5°, Midships. Steady as she goes.'

The Captain deftly turned his boat and aimed the submarine directly at the *Sagittario*. He was now on course for a head-on clash. George snapped into his own training procedures, and warned the crew to prepare for a collision and secure loose gear. (The doors were already shut as they were at 'Collision Stations'.)

At the same instant, there was a sickening, grating sound as metal wrenched on metal; the submarine shuddered. The two vessels crashed into each other's flanks and scraped along the entire length of both ships.

A submarine has two forward hydroplanes protruding from either side of the vessel, primarily designed to assist with changing depth by simply turning up or down. They also help with trim. They are joined to each other by an axle, or trunion, so that they work in concert, and are attached to the pressure hull by bolts.

With the force of the smash, the port hydroplane gashed right along the side of the destroyer, much as a can-opener would slice into a can. And, as George subsequently discovered, it broke off and fell into its engine room. The starboard hydroplane snapped off and became wedged in the submarine casing. Immediately, solid bars of water sluiced through the holes where the bolts had been sheared off and began to fill the forward tube space with ocean water.

Within seconds, the doors to the tube space were shut, containing the water in that compartment. Powerful water pumps roared into life. George quickly realized there was something wrong with the hydroplanes when they did not respond; they would have to dive by solely using the aft hydroplanes.

Peter Scott-Maxwell, the Engineer Officer, came forward at the double and said to George, 'We shouldn't dive until I find out what's going on. I'll nip forward and find out what the problem is.'

In an emergency, the tube-space doors would remain shut and the bow would become full of water, compromising their ability to dive. An inspection was worth the risk. Within a few seconds, Maxwell returned and reported, 'The hydroplanes are knocked out and large bars of water are pouring through the bolt holes. I'll get back to the engine room, and we'll produce some bungs and try and stop the flow.'

The tube-space doors were shut again while the Engineer returned to his men in the engine room and they began to gather some wooden bungs. He briskly returned with some of his men, opened the doors and pushed his way through the quickly accumulating water, his men following. They then hammered the bungs in place as a temporary measure and retreated. With the mission accomplished, the Captain stood down the gun crew and descended down to the control room. The destroyer, in the meantime, had disappeared into the dark to assess the situation.

Some time later, when it became obvious the destroyer had 'retired hurt', the ERA (Engine Room Artificer) took out the bungs and replaced them from the outside. This would allow the water pressure to push them in further. Then the Captain called up the voice pipe to the bridge and told the OOW to dive the boat. The Captain said to George, 'We'll go to periscope depth.'

The drama wasn't over yet as the submarine was still very heavy in the forward section with the extra weight in the tube space. Further, because of the damage to the forward hydroplanes, George was experiencing difficulty maintaining trim. The pumps in the forward tube space were running at full speed, and it took a concerted effort to keep the bow up and the submarine stable.

To dive, George still had control of his aft hydroplanes. He angled these to cock the stern up before increasing the speed, and the boat submerged.

It took a week of concentrated seamanship, carried out patiently and skilfully, for the crippled submarine to hobble home finally to

Alexandria and to berth alongside HMS *Medway*. Interestingly, the submarine on which *Proteus* berthed had suffered an internal fire among the batteries – a serious one. Because they were sister submarines, the *Proteus* was able to receive the other submarine's hydroplanes. It would not be long before the *Proteus* would be in action again.

However, George would not be in her. He had received orders to fly to Portsmouth in March 1942. He had been recommended and accepted by the Flag Officer Submarines to undertake the Commanding Officers' Qualifying Course which would enable him to be Captain of a submarine. The vision of a 12-year-old boy standing on the bridge of his own ship was about to materialize.

CHAPTER FIVE

First Command

The journey back to England was an adventure in itself. In the early part of the war, when the main opposition were the Italians in the Mediterranean, it was possible to fly to the United Kingdom fairly directly and unchallenged. However, once the Germans strengthened their presence, they set up efficient spy networks, rendering this situation unsafe.

As such, anybody now needing to go to England would have to travel in plain clothes, as a civilian, via a long route through Africa, neutral Portugal and Ireland. As naval personnel weren't routinely issued with a passport, this meant George firstly had to secure one. He was making the journey with a good friend from another submarine, Barry Charles, who was also flying home for his CO's course. When they applied for their passports, in order to obscure their naval background, they had to 'fudge' their professions. As George had a beard, he wrote down that he was a commercial artist and Barry put down that he was an architect.

When the Consul-General in Alexandria duly presented them with their passports, he asked, 'Which of you is Barry Charles?'

Charles replied, 'I am Sir.'

'Well,' he said with a droll smile, 'I advise you to learn how to spell "architect" before you continue on your journey. Luckily, Mr Hunt can spell "Commercial Artist" – he'll be alright.'

The first part of the journey took them by rail from Alexandria to Cairo. This trip was always interesting as they were suddenly confronted with the magnitude of the Western Desert. To George, in some ways, the moods of the desert and the ocean were similar. The vastness of both could trigger emotions of respect and awe, while at other times, both could evoke an innate sense of poetry, tranquillity and timelessness.

The train journey continued south from Cairo as it followed the course of the mighty Nile through to Khartoum in the Sudan. George was interested in this for here was where his Uncle George (the civil engineer) had been Head of the Gordon College of Engineering at Omdurman, across the river from Khartoum.

From his carriage window, George caught glimpses of antiquity as peasants tilled the soil with primitive tools and feluccas skimmed over the waters as they must have done for thousands of years. As they trundled past tantalizing archaeological sites revealing ancient pillars and pylons, he marvelled at the sight of monumental statues to long-forgotten gods, still demanding homage – testimony to a sophisticated civilization that once existed there and relied on the rhythm of life brought by the Nile.

At Khartoum, the men boarded a twin-engined Douglas DC3 in which all the seats had been removed and the fuselage was laden with mailbags. They quickly sprawled over the mailbags and made themselves comfortable. From here, they followed a mail run as they dropped in on El Fasher in western Sudan, Fort Lamy at Lac Tchad in the Chad Territory, and Maiduguri and Kano in Nigeria. At Kano, they spent the night sleeping on camp beds on the airfield. Finally they had a few days break at Lagos, the capital of Nigeria, where they were allowed to use the BOAC 'club' or canteen and its swimming pool.

From Lagos, they travelled in a degree of comfort in a Boeing Clipper, a flying boat complete with beds and bunks. The Clipper landed at Lisbon in Portugal where they spent the night, before continuing in another flying boat, an Empire-class, to Shannon in the Irish Free State. The Irish Free State was neutral and George was challenged again on his passport on arrival. A very severe-looking immigration officer looked hard at George and said, 'So you're a commercial artist?'

'Yes,' replied George, a little nervously.

The official broke into a big grin when he handed the passport back. In a strong Irish brogue, he said, 'Sure, an' I have a brother in the Royal Navy too. And I hear our lad Montgomery is doing a grand job. I believe he's a general now. Did you ever meet him?'

From here, it was a short hop back to Poole in England, then it was only about 40 miles (65 kilometres) to Portsmouth. In all, the journey took about two weeks and George revelled in the opportunity to travel.

George began the Commanding Officers' Course at the end of March 1942. It used to be called the Periscope Course, but now it was known simply as 'The Perisher'. The course, at this stage was run from the 'Alma Mater' for submarines, HMS *Dolphin* at Portsmouth, a place George knew well. There were ten submarines in the flotilla. Having been away for nine months, George was glad to be reunited with Phoebe. They had both been under fire and the time was precious.

On the first day of the course, George was informed that, basically, he would be taught to take command of a submarine under any circumstances. He was reminded that the submarine was a lethal weapon and that its two main strengths were torpedoes and mine-laying. Unlike the German U-boat commanders who were trained to hunt as a pack and to search for large convoys, British submarine Captains were trained to be able to act individually, sometimes poking in to harbours and fjords, landing agents and carrying out many unusual tasks.

It should be borne in mind that each pupil had already served several years in submarines, including time as First Lieutenant (second-in-command) of a submarine in war. He would also have been recommended by his Captain. So now he was to build on that experience and absorb the finer and important details.

They would be taught to penetrate a screen of enemy destroyers and seek out vital targets in a convoy without getting rammed or sunk themselves. To achieve this, while remaining unseen and undetected, the CO had to use the periscope very sparingly, yet retain in his head a clear picture, properly oriented, of every vessel in his vicinity.

As the course progressed, the applicants were taught primarily to gauge their enemy and plan their attack through the periscope. The first task was to identify their target – the type of ship. All categories of ships – marine or naval – were recorded on charts or books which would sometimes help them to assess the height of the funnel or mast quickly, which then allows the Captain to estimate the range. The second task was to measure the angle they were at, relevant to the enemy's bow, to predict his course. Correct identification would also allow the Captain to select appropriate depth settings for his torpedoes. He would need to know his own speed, the speed of the target, the speed of the torpedo and the distance from the target. He could then compute where to aim his torpedoes and when to fire. During all this, he would rely on his First Lieutenant and other members of the crew to keep the boat steady and in good trim. His Asdic operators would also be telling him, among other things, the number of revolutions of the enemy ship's propellers.

To aim for the best outcome he would need to co-ordinate and build a strong team spirit among the many skilled men throughout the boat. He would be particularly reliant on his officers who would help to note and plot all the relevant measurements, readings and bearings.

To gain a fuller perspective through the periscope, the Captain must be aware of the larger scene, such as the presence and position of any enemy escorts, or air support which might be protecting his target.

With training and skill in a snap attack, this decision-making process from first sighting to firing a torpedo might take as little as three minutes. At other times, depending on the situation, it could take a great deal longer as the Captain looked for a better position. If he had the luxury of being able to track his target silently, it might even take an hour or more to get into the best position. All this, while remaining unseen and undetected throughout.

The other aspect of the course that George found interesting was the business of laying mines. The most successful mines were not the spherical ones that floated near the surface, covered in horns, but mines that lie on the sea bed. Such mines could be laid from a submarine's torpedo tubes, looked more like oil drums and could be detonated by four mechanisms: the pressure of a ship passing over it; by magnetism, the magnets in the mine being altered by the magnetism of a ship passing over it; by the sound of a ship passing over it; and finally, by a simple clock which could be set to go off at a certain time.

As with all military weapons, George learned the tactics adopted by minesweepers to counter such mines. Naval and Merchant Navy vessels, in particular, would generally be 'degaussed' to offer protection against magnetic mines. This process involved running a large cable around a ship, attached to a generator, which induced a strong current that would negate the magnetism of the ship. To counter 'noise' mines, ships were fitted with noise-makers that went 'bang, bang, bang' – they were called Kango hammers – which would set off the mine before the ship passed over it.

George was absorbed by all aspects of the course, beginning gently with models, then using a periscope that was maintained in a static and controlled training establishment, and then finally, a number of exercises at sea in a submarine.

At the end of three months, George graduated as a Submarine Commanding Officer. The course had been difficult, with 15 per cent of the students failing. However, he now felt confident to take on his first command.

This was HMS *H33*. George took command in July 1942, joining her at Loch Long on the Firth of Clyde in Scotland. He was to take her down to Sheerness at the mouth of the Thames where she was to be put in dock for a refit. It was something of an anti-climax. He was all ready to sail at noon, but because of the low spring tide, the submarine was actually sitting on the bottom. He was finally able to leave at 3.00pm. It was a simple enough task but it cut the ice for him. At Sheerness, he took over command of *H50* which had been refitted and was ready for service again.

H50 had been built during the First World War and was a very simple submarine. She was therefore straightforward and reliable, and George was pleased for his first real command to cut his teeth on her.

He was pleasantly surprised to find that his First Lieutenant was a New Zealander, Lieutenant Con Thode RNZNVR who he knew well as they had served together recently in HMS *Proteus*, commanded by Phillip Francis. On that boat, George had been the First Lieutenant and Thode the Navigating Officer.

In the meantime, George was delighted to hear that he was to receive a decoration, reported in the *London Gazette* of 30 June 1942. He had been awarded the Distinguished Service Cross (DSC) for gallant and distinguished service in successful patrols while serving in HMS *Proteus*. This was great news and a good cause for celebrations. The highlight was to attend the investiture at Buckingham Palace in July to be presented with his award by King George VI. It was particularly pleasing as both Phoebe and one of his aunts could also attend this most memorable occasion.

George took over command of *H50* in August and undertook several tasks over the next few months. These mainly involved *H50* being used as a 'clockwork mouse' for destroyers that were learning to use Asdic and hunt submarines, before they went on Atlantic convoys and joined their submarine hunting groups. He did, however, carry out several war patrols in her in the North Sea and Bay of Biscay.

By the end of October, George knew he was ready for what would be his first major active command.

CHAPTER SIX

HMS *Ultor*

George's new orders were to 'stand by' the building of a new submarine at Vickers Armstrong at Barrow in Furness. He had fulfilled this exercise before, with the *Urchin* (renamed the *Sokol*), for the Poles, but this time he was to be the new Captain. He was very enthusiastic about this project and he and Phoebe moved to Barrow and settled into pleasant 'digs'.

His submarine was numbered *P53*. However, much earlier in the war, Churchill had decided that all submarines should have a name. As the new vessel was one of the Unity-class – or U-class – submarines, the name had to start with 'U'.

George happened to know someone who was the Somerset Herald in the College of Heralds and so when he asked for his advice, the reply was, 'Why not call it *Ultor*, from the full title of "Mars Ultor", the Roman God of War? There is actually a temple still standing in Rome in the Forum of Augustus dedicated to "Mars *Ultor*". He was the "God" who avenged the death of Julius Caesar. It's certainly appropriate.'

George submitted the name through the Flag Officer Submarines and the Admiralty readily approved the name.

George was very comfortable with the U-class boats. He had, after all, been rammed and sunk in one, *Unity*, and he did have the earlier experiences with the *Urchin*. He therefore approached the project enthusiastically. Initially, he spent time meticulously studying the final stages of building and then started putting together a crew. He knew what sort of men he wanted, as the Unity-class boats were different in many aspects to larger submarines. However, he was well aware that the final choice would be in the hands of those who had to juggle the drafting and appointments.

Selection of a crew was made a little easier as, before being chosen for service in submarines, most seamen had already been trained for specialist duties such as torpedo, gunnery, engineering and communications in the naval schools. All had already fulfilled a six-week submarine course at the Fifth Flotilla, Fort Blockhouse at Gosport, and some had already experienced extensive submarine duties and war patrols. Ultimately, George was pleased with the crew he finally received.

The U-class submarines were not originally designed as operational vessels but were intended to serve the Navy more as 'clockwork mice' in the training of warships in anti-submarine detectors. However, because of the impending war situation, the first ones built in 1937 were immediately given an operational role, and quickly proceeded to excel, especially in the Mediterranean.

Their smaller size made them ideal for a commanding officer's first operational command, although as a fighting vessel the U-class had some minor disadvantages. They could only attain a maximum speed of 10 knots, which was woefully inadequate. This meant they often had little chance to catch up with or overtake a merchant ship, and practically no chance of out-manoeuvring an enemy warship, situations which often called for creative, strategic leadership from their Captains.

The living conditions were more cramped than usual. The boat required thirty-two to thirty-six crew, including three or four officers, and, at only 500 tons, conditions on board were sometimes overcrowded, especially when landing specialist parties, such as Royal Marines.

The early U-class boats also suffered from possessing an almost totally useless 12-pounder gun. However, now that the two external bulbous tubes had been removed, a more effective 3-inch gun was mounted on the casing in front of the bridge instead. The submarine's size limited them to only eight torpedoes, four of which could be fired in one salvo. Their size also restricted their patrols to about a fortnight and to a range of 500 miles (800 kilometres). On the plus side, as has already been mentioned, they could dive with unmatched speed – a well-trained crew could submerge the vessel in about sixteen seconds.

One of the qualities George was looking for in his men was tolerance, which they would need in buckets. By the time he sailed, George had the confidence that the men who finally comprised his crew would be endowed with the necessary training, intellect and psychological character suitable for submarine life and warfare.

He found he was fortunate with the quality of his officers. As they could be at sea for an indefinite period, he needed to respect and trust these men. He was therefore delighted to have once more as his First Lieutenant, Lieutenant Con Thode, who had not only been his First Lieutenant in *H50*, but they had previously served together in HMS *Proteus*.

Lieutenant Barry Rowe joined as his Navigating Officer and impressed George from the very start. He came from a strong naval background, his father having served in the Navy in the First World War and Rowe himself was trained at the Royal Naval College, Dartmouth. He had already served in various submarines.

The Armament Officer was a quietly-spoken, highly efficient and very likable young man, Lieutenant Neville Mangnall. He had been a solicitor in private life but had also joined the RNVR and volunteered for submarines.

The Coxswain, Chief Petty Officer Harry Armstrong, had also joined the crew. He and the First Lieutenant virtually ran the ship between them, being responsible for, among other things, the discipline and morale of the men.

Over some weeks during 'acceptance trials', the three officers and the Coxswain worked on a programme for knocking the ship's company into shape. The period was used to develop and mould an efficient, dedicated and responsive team. By the time they had finished these trials from the builder's yard and they were ready for their first patrol, George felt he had the makings of an effective and cohesive man-of-war. There was to be a 'working-up' patrol off

Murmansk in Russia in January 1943.

But before that, Phoebe was awarded a singular courtesy on her birthday, 23 December. She was given the honour of launching the T-class submarine *P317*, HMS *Tally Ho* – a most memorable occasion. The new T-class boats were larger vessels and could remain at sea for a period of some six weeks.

At this stage of the war, Britain and the United States were sending large convoys to assist their embattled ally, Russia. These convoys gathered near the Arctic Circle off Iceland, then travelled north of Norway and on to Murmansk – 'the Arctic Convoys'. The convoys were always under threat of attack by large German battleships lurking in the Norwegian fjords, including the *Tirpitz* and the *Emden*, while German U-boats were actively aggressive in their efforts to maul the convoys.

The *Ultor* reached the region in early January. No one was really prepared for what was in store for them. The conditions could not have been more atrocious. It was mid-winter, freezing cold and as the sun was below the horizon day and night it was pitch black. George's covering patrol position was off North Cape, Norway, at approximately 72° N., an area which was miserable any time of the year, but now was infinitely worse. The patrol was memorable for the mountainous seas, swirling snow, stinging hail squalls and horizontally driven rain, set under a morbid curtain of black cloud and sky that seemed infinite.

George had always been aware that the ocean is a place where the natural order of things prevails overwhelmingly – known as the 'Whispers of the Sea'. But this was no whisper – it was a roar.

The OOW would tie a belt round his waist and clip it to a rail running round the inside of the bridge to ensure his safety. When *Ultor* surfaced to recharge her batteries, shrieking wind blasts ripped sheets of water off the ocean. Shattered shards of spray were sent crashing onto the conning tower, the water turning to ice the moment it hit the bridge. Within seconds the outer hull resembled an ice rink.

When the upper hatch was open, the ice would form so quickly on the rim that it would prevent the seat of the hatch from shutting cleanly. George had to place a sailor to sit there with a hammer. His mission was to chip the ice away continually as it formed so that the hatch would fit securely on its rubber seating when the boat dived. A canvas bath was rigged in the control room to catch the water which rushed over the bridge and down the conning tower.

As the days lengthened into a second week, the miserable conditions were beginning to reflect on crew morale. What increased the difficulty was that the sailors had not been issued with appropriate foul-weather clothing. Once again, George was amazed at the lack of foresight of those responsible for such matters. Worse, during the next two and a half weeks, they didn't sight another ship. George was aware his crew were exasperated and on edge, although privately, with the responsibility of being Captain, he considered he was probably more stressed than anybody.

It was a testing environment for any individual and every man was grateful when the patrol was finished. Spirits began to soar as the *Ultor* finally headed south to Lerwick in the Shetland Isles to refuel. The experience would serve to strengthen their resolve.

On their return from that miserable and unforgettable patrol, there was a change in personnel. Con Thode left the *Ultor* to take up his appointment on the 'Perisher' course, his place as First Lieutenant being taken by a Lieutenant Fovarque whom George had never met. As Fovarque had not previously served in a U-class submarine, George hoped the passage to Malta would give him a chance to familiarize himself with the boat and to get to know the crew.

CHAPTER SEVEN

Algiers

George took the *Ultor* through familiar territory down the Strait of Gibraltar and out into the warm waters of the Mediterranean. Since he was last there, the situation in the Middle East had changed dramatically. The Eighth Flotilla, which had been based at Gibraltar, had been transferred, complete with its mother ship *Maidstone*, to Algiers, the capital of Algeria, in November 1942. Algeria bordered on Tunisia where the remnants of the now retreating Afrika Korps were preparing for a last stand. Rommel had been beaten in Egypt, delivering a significant victory to the Allies in October 1942 at the Battle of El Alamein. His army had been pushed back through Libya and was now standing in disarray on the north-east corner of Tunisia.

George noted, with some irony and satisfaction, how the fortunes of war had changed so completely. Whereas Rommel had been instrumental in driving the British Expeditionary Force onto the beaches of Dunkirk three years earlier, the positions were now reversed. This time, however, the Germans had little chance to be evacuated for the seas were now dominated by the Allies.

Rommel had fought bitter battles against Montgomery's Eighth Army in Egypt and Libya, and the British and the Americans in Tunisia, but he was now back in Germany, sick and disillusioned. He had been relieved by General Sixt von Arnim, but neither of them had been able to mount any attacks without petrol, food and ammunition, the bulk of which had been sunk by Allied submarines and aircraft operating from Malta.

George berthed on HMS *Maidstone* at Algiers in early April 1943, and was soon given his first patrol. This was supposed to be a 'quiet' patrol away from the 'hot' cauldron area of Malta. (Malta was still central to the Allies' quest to prevent enemy supplies reaching the Afrika Korps in Tunisia.) The *Ultor* set out towards the French Riviera not expecting much action, but as it was his first truly operational command, George took a very serious view of his mission.

By now the crew were used to their cramped facilities. As already mentioned, a U-class boat was not designed for comfort. The junior sailors (rates) slept in hammocks swinging between torpedo racks in the torpedo stowage compartment. The only bunks were in the wardroom and Senior Rates' Mess.

For U-class boats, periscope depth was reached when the top of the periscope standards were 10 or 12 feet below the surface – this occured when the depth gauge showed about 20 feet (6 metres). Every thirty seconds or thereabouts, the periscope was raised to about 6 inches or a foot above the surface. The OOW had a quick look around the horizon and also in the air space above – for about five to ten seconds. His left hand controlled the lens, moving it from high power to low, while the right hand controlled the angle of vision – up or down. If nothing caught his eye, he might have stayed up for a few more seconds.

For a periscope search, the OOW would signal (by hand) for the periscope to be raised, or he would call, 'Up periscope.' He would then have a quick all-round scan for five to ten seconds before signalling 'Down periscope.'

Towards the evening of 12 April, the *Ultor* was off Cape Camarat, a headland which juts into the Mediterranean a few kilometres from St Tropez. The submarine had been patrolling routinely at periscope depth and the OOW was alert. However, at 7.00pm, as darkness was closing, George decided to surface and start charging the batteries. It was a pleasant enough night with the weather conditions calm. The sky was generally overcast and George noted a fitful moon as it raced in and out behind the clouds. At 10.30pm, through the shadows, the OOW briefly thought he saw a cluster of three ships and called

George to the bridge. With mounting excitement, George realized he had seen an enemy destroyer and two smaller merchant vessels. Reacting swiftly, he ordered, 'Diving Stations'. ('Diving Stations' is an order that directs the crew to the positions for diving, surfacing or an attack.) Men moved quickly to their stations, awaiting further directions. Adrenalin pumped. George ordered the torpedo tube crew, 'Bring all tubes to the "action state".' This order includes blowing water in to the torpedo tube to fill the space surrounding the torpedo. George then brought the boat to within 3,000 yards of the two merchant vessels. Deftly, he manoeuvred the boat until both of the merchant vessels were in his firing line, keeping his distance from the destroyer.

At the same time, various officers relayed data to him. George asked the Navigating Officer, or the 'Pilot' as he was traditionally called, 'What do you make the enemy course, Pilot?'

By now, the Pilot had plotted the enemy ships' bearing and distance and suggested their approximate course and speed. (This plotting was achieved by pencil, paper and parallel rulers, and practised use of geometry, mental arithmetic and, in the case of a snap attack, an intelligent 'guesstimate'.) The Asdic operators had also been listening to the enemy ships' propeller count to give an idea of speed and reported that it was eighty revolutions a minute.

Surprise was still on their side. When he was confident everything was in order he warned the torpedo tubes crew, 'Stand by.' (At this order bow caps would be opened, if not previously ordered.)

George ordered for the torpedoes' depth settings to be set at 8 and 10 feet. Their 'spread' was to be 600 feet (180 metres), twice the length of one of the enemy ships. ('Spread' is the distance between the first and last torpedo. 'Spreading' the torpedoes makes some allowance for errors in estimating the course and speed of the target.)

After a last-minute consultation with the Pilot, Asdics and the First Lieutenant, George issued a final warning, 'Stand by.'

At 10.55pm, all conditions were right. George called, 'Stand by number one tube – Fire!'

He then repeated this command for tubes two, three and four at twelve-second intervals. He was now confident his four 'fish' would be racing towards their targets at 45 knots and at 200 feet distance from each other. For a few seconds, George watched the dark waters where the torpedoes trailed off towards the merchant vessels.

At 11.01, the crew were rewarded as the first torpedo slammed into one enemy vessel. Their cheers were drowned as, twelve seconds later, the second torpedo smashed into the same vessel, setting off another distant explosion. Exactly twenty-five seconds later, a third torpedo connected with the second vessel. As further muffled explosions echoed back to the ebullient crew of the *Ultor*, George ordered the OOW to press the diving klaxon, before saying to the First Lieutenant, 'We'll go to 200 feet, shut off for depth charges and go to silent routine.'

Key crewmen skilfully opened the vents of the ballast tanks to let the compressed air out and the water in. The submarine submerged and waited at 200 feet (61 metres) of water – no noise or movement – in complete silence. A dropped tool could be heard by an experienced enemy Asdic operator.

The crew of the *Ultor* waited in silence – ten minutes, twenty minutes. To their relief no depth charges were forthcoming. After waiting a bit longer, George gave the necessary orders for the boat to creep away slowly from the scene of the crime. Common sense dictated that there was no merit in moving quickly or loudly. The escort must not be alerted to their position or status – they would quietly melt away.

There was great excitement all around. This was their first victory – two 3,000-ton vessels would no longer be supporting the enemy's cause.

The crew of the *Ultor* did not have long to wait to get a chance to maintain their exhilaration. Having reloaded the torpedo tubes, the next day, the 13th, was spent in good spirits. However, as the sun rose on the morning of the 14th, it revealed more than a beautiful, bright and sunny Mediterranean day.

The *Ultor* was now just east of Toulon and, through the periscope, the sun fairly shimmered off the water. At 7.25am, George's interest was triggered as another merchant vessel crystallized into view. He quickly noted its silhouette and consulted his Talbot-Booth's book.

This very useful publication lists most big shipping companies and identifies ships by scale drawings. He had at least half a dozen of these 'recognition' type books, including *Jane's Fighting Ships*.

It was the 2,200-ton French vessel, *Penerf*. Its escort was bobbing on the water some distance from it – not the traditional destroyer, but an Italian flying boat, a Cant Z501, a reconnaissance bomber biplane. They could be dangerous, but George moved the *Ultor* in to 3,200 yards from the vessel in preparation for firing.

Once again, he ordered the torpedo crew, 'Bring all torpedoes to action state.'

It made sense to spread the four torpedoes across the target, one ahead, two midships and one astern. At exactly 7.51am, with a firing interval of fifteen seconds, he fired the four torpedoes.

The crew waited expectantly. Two minutes and forty-five seconds later, the tension yielded to cheers. Three quick successive explosions, twenty seconds apart ripped through the *Penerf* – three direct hits. The fourth torpedo hit the beach a few kilometres away. The *Penerf* sank to the bottom in 400 fathoms of water.

Once again, there was great exhilaration among the crew. The 'quiet' patrol had been anything but. As Captain, George derived great satisfaction at his 'First Blood'.

That was the *Ultor's* only patrol from Algiers. At the end of April, the boat was transferred to the Tenth Flotilla at Malta – where the real action was.

CHAPTER EIGHT

Malta

The *Ultor* arrived at Malta on 2 May, 1943. George knew the island reasonably well having visited it before the war, and again recently in 1941 during his first tour of duty to the Mediterranean. At that stage, the island had been receiving a consistent battering ever since the Italians had placed Malta under siege in September 1940, when General Graziani commenced his invasion of Egypt from Libya. George noticed that conditions were now considerably worse.

Before the war, right back to the 1800s, Malta had been a key British overseas naval base, being annexed to Britain in 1814. There was now a sizeable British Army presence there; as well as the active submarine flotilla, it included three airfields manned by heroic and hard-pressed air crew and ground staff. The Air Force contingent was mainly flying Beaufighters, Albacores, Spitfires, Hurricanes, Blenheims and Wellingtons, while the Fleet Air Arm flew Swordfish. (This was a vast improvement since 1940–1 when Malta's air defence consisted solely of three Gladiators, optimistically named 'Faith, Hope and Charity'.)

In the early years of the siege, the Italians had bombed the island relentlessly, taking off from air bases in Sicily. Then in the early months of 1942, when Germany came to Italy's assistance, Malta was bombed so intensively – virtually daily – it appeared to the enemy that there was nothing left to destroy. In fact, by September, the island was so close to starvation and low on supplies that the Governor of Malta considered capitulation. Indeed, to the casual observer, the Grand Harbour and Valletta, the capital, appeared to be seriously crippled, as over 30,000 buildings had been very badly damaged.

However, remarkably, most of the systems and infrastructure were still in place; the Maltese people and their British protectors had rallied magnificently against this adversity. Britain's main objective was to keep Malta operational as an unsinkable aircraft carrier and an invaluable submarine base.

The Tenth Flotilla Submarine Base was at Manoel Island, Lazaretto Creek, to the north of Valletta, to which it was attached via a causeway. The rest of the large Mediterranean Fleet had recently been moved to Alexandria in Egypt.

The submarine base itself, HMS *Talbot*, was created around the strongly-built stone building of what was a former leper hospital called Lazaretto. It now possessed a little underground living and storage quarter, and engineering workshops, but not nearly enough.

Towards the end of 1942, owing to the intensive bombing and the fact that two submarines had been damaged by it, it had been decided that when a boat returned from patrol, two-thirds of the ship's company would come ashore into the base while the remainder took the boat out into deep water and simply dived to a safe depth. They would then sit on the bottom and carry out minor repairs and adjustments, and some cleaning until it was dark, when they would surface and berth on Lazaretto for repairs to proceed overnight.

In the meantime, in Valletta, the people used the catacombs under the city and took refuge down among the remains of their ancestors. They made excellent air-raid shelters. The irony of all this, however, was that before the war the authorities had actually started to excavate three tunnels in the cliffs just across the water from Lazaretto. These tunnels were to be shelters for submarines which would be able to move into them while afloat. Perhaps the money ran out, but although the project was started, it was stopped at a point where the excavations, as far as they had gone, were of no use to anyone.

The mainstay of the submarine flotilla was constructed around the strength of mainly U-class boats, the first of which arrived in January

1941, the *Upholder*. On the day George arrived, there were twelve U-class boats in action from there. (The S-class submarines were based at Algiers in the Eighth Flotilla and the larger submarines of the T and older classes were based first at Alexandria and later at Beirut, in the First Flotilla.)

George was always interested in Malta's history. A conflict of epic proportions was not new to the inhabitants, for this was the second great siege the island had withstood. Even though its land size was small, having an area of only 120 square miles, because of its position it had been fought over since the Phoenicians plied their Mediterranean trade ships in 800 BC. It was eventually absorbed into the Roman Empire about 200 BC but was converted to Christianity by the Apostle Paul in AD 60. Since then, during the Middle Ages, Muslims and Crusaders fought many bloody battles over the precious piece of rock and dirt. In 1565, the Grand Master, Jean Vallete, head of the Knights of St John, held off a siege against Suleiman the Magnificent for four terrible months – the first Great Siege of Malta. When Napoleon tried to take the island in 1800 and was turned around by Nelson's fleet, after its victory at the Battle of the Nile, Malta clamoured to join the British Empire.

As the *Ultor* secured to the moorings close to the southern walls of Lazaretto, which rose sheer from the water's edge, George could immediately see the devastating results of the continual bombardment. The walls and surrounding buildings were pock-marked from incessant attacks. Other buildings were lying in ruins, the result of exploding bombs and aircraft machine-gun fire.

George's crew were bunked on the mess deck of Lazaretto and George shared a room with another submarine CO, Bruce Andrew, Captain of the *Unbroken*. There were shortages of everything – even the glasses in the mess were sawn-off beer bottles, the end result of a process where a red-hot wire is drawn over the bottle. The *Ultor* crew spent a few days storing and refuelling, and having a quiet rest before preparing for their second Mediterranean patrol.

One of the important ceremonies the crew took part in at this stage was to celebrate with their 'success flag' – the infamous 'Jolly Roger'. The tradition for a submarine to hoist a Jolly Roger, normally taken to be a black flag with a white skull and crossbones emblazoned on it and associated with pirates, began in the First World War. After sinking a German cruiser and destroyer in September 1914, Lieutenant Commander Max Horton, the Captain of HM submarine *E9* returned to base flying a Jolly Roger. The adoption as a 'success flag' proudly flown on return from a successful patrol stems from that time.

As the *Ultor* achieved her first successes, the record with suitable symbols was sewn on by the signalman. (The most usual symbols were a white bar for a merchant ship, red for a warship, stars for successful gun actions, a lighthouse for acting as a navigation beacon during an amphibious landing and a dagger for a special operation, such as landing or recovering an agent.)

As already mentioned, the war for General von Arnim and his Afrika Korps was not going well. They were now under siege in Tunisia with little hope of being evacuated; not a single supply ship had managed to get through since 19 April. On 8 May, Admiral Sir Andrew Cunningham, the Allied Commander of the Expeditionary Force and Commander-in-Chief of the Mediterranean Fleet, signalled the start of Operation RETRIBUTION with the words 'Sink, burn and destroy. Let nothing pass.' Such was the pressure, von Arnim surrendered his almost 250,000 troops on 13 May.

The scent of the victory was heady stuff. Malta could now breathe easier. General Alexander, Commander of the Middle East campaign in Egypt, signalled to Churchill: 'We are masters of the North African Shores.' Now the Allies could concentrate on taking the fight to Italy.

Virtually overnight, after a siege of almost three years, Malta was converted from a beleaguered fortress to a base for attack. D-Day for Allied landings in Sicily – Operation HUSKY – would be 10 July 1943. Troops, tanks, guns and ships were already converging to the Mediterranean. As a result, the Tenth Flotilla was earmarked for a renewed assault on enemy shipping in the Tyrrhenian Sea, north of Sicily, as well as carrying out specialist beach reconnaissance sorties, and landing and recovering agents.

By mid-May, the *Ultor*, along with the other Us which included two Polish boats, were aggressively patrolling the seas off Sicily and the west coast of Italy. Scores were quickly racked up. On the 16th, *Unruly* torpedoed an armed merchant cruiser. *Unbroken*, under the command of Lieutenant Bruce Andrew, George's room-mate at Lazaretto, sank a tug on the 19th and the next day destroyed the 5,140-ton *Bologna*.

George started off his patrol in *Ultor* with some frustration. After scouring down the east coast of Calabria, on the toe of Italy, all he found was a hospital ship and some Swedish relief ships bound for Greece. However, his opportunity for action came during the early morning of the 23rd after the *Ultor* had been patrolling along Sicily's east coast. The sea was glassy calm, the sky clear; it was a beautiful day. While moving at periscope depth, George could clearly see the outline of the fabled volcano, Mt Etna, towering above the coastline. He then moved south to a position just off the harbour of Port Augusta.

To approach a harbour like this was always a dangerous proposition. Many entrances to harbours in this area were mined and George had no information whether Augusta Harbour had a boom net or any mines guarding it. Gingerly, he took the *Ultor* towards the harbour entrance. There was no clear sign of a boom. Then, through the periscope, he saw that the area was guarded by an anti-submarine trawler, or UJ-boat. These ships were specifically designed to attack submarines. George sighted the vessel where it had stopped beside a buoy at the entrance to the harbour. He estimated its tonnage at about 800, with a draft of about 12 feet. It would be his next target.

He could hear the trawler's anti-submarine Asdic pinging madly so there would be no doubt that they knew there was a submarine close. (Submarines don't continually 'ping' searching for vessels as they would give themselves away. In fact, they rarely transmit any signal, by Asdic, radio or radar – they need to remain silent so they mainly listen on their hydrophones. The vessels which usually emit a 'ping' are destroyers and anti-submarine vessels searching for submarines.)

Timing was now critical. George envisaged that at this moment the crew on the trawler would be scrambling like mad to get their vessel under way, giving him a few seconds' advantage. He would have to act quickly if he intended to hit the vessel while it was stationary. One torpedo would do it. George searched the seas and sky briskly and could find no escort. Calmly, like a lion stalking its prey, George took the *Ultor* in closer and ordered the torpedo depth setting to be 6 feet. Everything was right. At 8.21am he fired the torpedo, aiming directly amidships of the trawler.

As the torpedo shot out of the tube, George felt very slight pressure on his ears. He still could not see an escort, so he stayed at periscope depth for a couple of minutes and watched the path of the 'fish' as it ran towards the luckless trawler. Everyone held their breath. Fifty-eight seconds later the torpedo exploded into the ship, breaking its back, the impact being accompanied by a shattering explosion. A red fireball angrily twisted and encompassed the ship in palls of thick, black smoke.

Satisfied with his attack, George knew it would not take long for assistance to race onto the scene. It was time to get out.

The *Ultor* planed down quickly to 200 feet and went into silent routine. George and his crew felt reasonably secure, not having sighted an escort. However, after a few minutes, the men were a little shocked to hear a sudden explosion – somebody was dropping depth charges around them and they were not too far away. There must have been an E-boat lurking somewhere. The submarine trembled mildly, but the explosions caused no real damage. Then the crew heard more thumping, closer this time, followed by further mild shock waves. Most of the crew had already experienced depth-charge attacks earlier in other boats; however, for three or four men, it was their first baptism of fire. To some, it would be a test but they had been trained for this.

In the cramped control room, George watched his men carefully. Around him were the Torpedo and Gunnery Officer, the Navigating Officer and the First Lieutenant, Lieutenant Fovarque. Fovarque was quietly giving orders to the two hydroplane operators in order to control the trim. The minutes crept by. To George's relief, no one showed any outward signs of fear. This would be a good crew – no weak links. He noted that some men reacted quite matter-of-factly, even blasé. All the same, he was obdurate that everyone treated any attack on the boat very seriously as a potential hazard, requiring professional treatment or action.

'He's getting closer!'

'No, that one was further away.'

In fact, some acted with bravado, even betting on the outcome.

'Two bob says the next one will be closer.'

'You're on.'

George counted the blasts. Fifteen depth charges in all were dropped around them, but to everyone's relief, they did not explode close enough to inflict any serious damage. After some time, George took the *Ultor* slowly and quietly out of harm's way. It had been a small but successful start.

Back at base, George found that May had been very productive for the Tenth Flotilla. As well as the victories already described, and his own, the Polish submarine *Dzik* had finished the month off by severely damaging the massive 12,000-ton *Carnaro*.

June would be even more fruitful.

CHAPTER NINE

Cape d'Orlando

On 1 June 1943, the Naval Commander-in-Chief, Sir Andrew Cunningham, had his command extended eastwards so that the whole of the central Mediterranean now came under his control. His three submarine flotillas would all be involved in Operation HUSKY. The Tenth Flotilla would be at the centre of the action. As the month began, some of the Tenth Flotilla submarines continued with reconnaissance and others fact-finding missions, but most searched for enemy vessels.

Before sailing, there were some more changes to *Ultor*. Unfortunately, Lieutenant Fovarque was suddenly recalled to the United Kingdom to undergo his 'Perisher', which was a little unsettling as the crew were beginning to mould into a fine team. Barry Rowe moved into the position of First Lieutenant and his place as Navigating Officer was taken by a young Belgian, Sub Lieutenant Charlie Pels.

Pels' father had been an official in the Belgian Government at the start of the war. Charlie, who had been attending university in Belgium, came to Britain with his father when the Belgian Government transferred to England. On arrival in Britain, Charlie joined the RNVR and volunteered for submarines. His English was impeccable, his manner charming and he fitted in very well.

There was one final 'shuffle'. The Coxswain, Chief Petty Officer Harry Armstrong, went sick and was put in hospital. His place was taken by the splendid, cheerful and effective Chief Petty Officer Claxton. Claxton was the senior non-commissioned officer on board and George amused himself by observing that 'Claxton' was a good name for a submariner – all submarines have a klaxon which calls the crew to 'Diving Stations' and to dive the boat. The entire ship's company was now able to settle down and concentrate on working as a harmonious and efficient team.

Ultor sailed from Malta on 6 June with George and his crew looking forward to their third Mediterranean patrol. The ocean would be a lot quieter than the incessant bombing endured in Malta. A few days later they were in position off Cape d'Orlando in northern Sicily. It was a brilliant midsummer's day; at noon, the sea was glassy and calm; visibility was excellent. The *Ultor* was at periscope depth and George could see a small naval auxiliary vessel (a petrol carrier) sailing into his view. It was moving steadily at about 12 knots in reasonably deep water of 64 fathoms. It displaced about 800 tons and had a draft of only 8 feet. It would be a worthwhile target.

George took the *Ultor* in closer, to 1,000 yards. He also ordered the torpedo crew to bring tubes one and two to the ready. He could see no escorts so he would aim one torpedo just abaft the bow and the other just ahead of the stern.

At 12.32, the torpedos flashed through the clear waters.

Unfortunately, the clear visibility worked against the *Ultor*. Even though the torpedoes were well below the surface, the enemy could clearly see their 'tracks' as the powerful harbingers of death, racing at 45 knots, churned the waters after them, signalling their presence and intention. The vessel instantly took effective avoiding action by altering course and turning away from the torpedo tracks. To George and the crew's frustration, both of the torpedoes missed, slicing through the water on either side of the ship. The beach was about 1,700 yards behind the carrier and, seventy seconds later, the torpedoes crashed into the foreshore.

The petrol carrier increased speed and raced away from the scene. George was debating whether he should surface and use his gun; however, hovering overhead, a menacing aerial escort arrived and convinced him to retire. He would wait for another day.

There was some small satisfaction two days later when George found the tail fin of a downed Italian aircraft floating in the ocean. On closer examination, most of the fuselage had sunk, but some gruesome pieces of the rear gunner were floating around the debris. George cut the Italian crest out of the tail as a souvenir.

The next day, the 13th, he found the ideal target to give his gun crew some practice. About 50 kilometres north of Sicily in the Lipari (Eolie) Archipelago, the *Ultor* came upon a wireless station on the shore of Salina Island. The facility was known as a wireless direction-finding station. George then ordered the Gunnery Officer, Lieutenant Mangnall, to have a good look at the target through the periscope. It was just after 9.00pm and there was barely enough light to make out a building and tall mast standing beside it.

George ordered, 'Gun action stations.'

He then brought *Ultor* closer to the target and surfaced about 2,000 yards from the beach. The gun crew scrambled up the conning tower and quickly prepared the gun for action. This was the *Ultor*'s first real gun action and the whole boat's crew was in high spirits.

On George's orders to the Gunnery Officer, the 3-inch gun roared into life, splitting the stillness of the peaceful island night. The inhabitants woke to a crack, followed by a whistling sound and a resounding crash. The first and second rounds landed close to the building, spraying up sand and dust. In quick succession, the third shell fell squarely on the target, shattering the mast. It crashed to the ground, crumpling in a heap next to some startled inhabitants who had raced out of the building. The event also raised cheers from *Ultor*'s crew as the results were relayed back to them.

The pounding continued as round after round landed on the building and the surrounding area. By now, local villagers, stirred by the noise, had found their way to the beach. They simply stared, with pardonable excitement, at the explosions, smoke and eventual devastation.

In all, the gun crew fired forty-three rounds and were very pleased with their high hit tally. The observable damage was certainly convincing. The station was well and truly put out of use, much of the mast and associated equipment being reduced to rubble. On completion George then dived the boat.

The *Ultor*, at periscope depth, continued to move east and, two days later, on the 15th, while searching just north of the Straits of Messina (which run between Sicily and the toe of Italy), George sighted his next intended victim. The day, as usual for this time of year, was fine and calm. At 1.40, in the lazy afternoon haze, while at periscope depth, George identified an Italian minelayer, the 1,200-ton *Tullio*. It was moving at about 9 knots, its clipper-shaped bow spraying water in a graceful arc. George would need some care – the vessel had escorts, two menacing Orsa-class destroyers of about 855 tons each, riding shotgun, one on either side.

George took the *Ultor* in to 1,000 yards and ordered three torpedoes to be brought to the ready. (For a torpedo to be 'brought to the ready', or 'to the action state', water had to be flooded into the tube around the torpedo. If, after a time, the torpedo was not fired, the tube was drained and the torpedo had to be pulled out of the tube to undertake a 'flooded routine' maintenance check.) He calculated he would need a wide spread and so would aim the first torpedo just ahead of the bow; the next two would follow at intervals across the target. He wasted no time and gave the order to fire.

Without waiting to see the outcome, George told Barry Rowe, 'Take her down to 200 feet, shut off for depth-charging and go to silent routine.' George knew the destroyers would react instantly. Fifty seconds later, the crew of the *Ultor* were delighted to hear a muffled explosion as one of the torpedoes hit its mark. But they weren't out of harm's way themselves.

Right on cue, a few minutes later, one depth charge exploded not too far away from them. Shock waves vibrated through the boat, but did no actual harm. The men braced themselves – more would be coming. They waited.

The moments ticked by. Nothing. Eventually the tension eased; no more depth charges were dropped.

George steadily and quietly moved out of the area and brought the *Ultor* to periscope depth. In the distance, he could see that the *Tullio* had gone; the two destroyers were milling around the scene. A thought formed in George's mind: it would be dangerous, but it would be good to notch up a destroyer as well. He would stalk them.

For the next five hours, George kept the *Ultor* at a respectable distance from the destroyers, which were of course still searching for the submarine as they moved around the Lipari Archipelago. At one stage, while waiting for an opportunity, they moved past Stromboli Island where George noticed belching columns of smoke rising from the island's active volcano.

Just on sunset, George took his chance. The seas were becoming choppy, but the visibility was still good. The destroyers presented a tempting target and, to his delight, one in particular came towards him. George commenced a head-on attack. Ranging on the destroyer, he determined its speed at 9 knots, which tied in with his Asdic's propeller count.

He had three torpedoes left so he ordered them to be brought to the action state, with depth settings of 6 feet. He had watched the destroyer as it made two alterations of course, and though not really a regular zigzag, he would have to incorporate that in his calculations. He would have to spread the salvo wisely. Also, at a range of 3,000 yards, he realized his chances of success were not great.

At 8.17pm, just as the light was fading, *Ultor* was on a 90-degree track angle, which tied in with the navigator's plot. George was ready. He fired the first torpedo a quarter length ahead of the stem (bow), the next one in the middle of his target and the third one abaft the stern. He immediately dived the *Ultor* to 200 feet and waited in silent routine. A few minutes later, he was rewarded by hearing an explosion at the correct timing interval, signifying the probability of a hit.

The crew knew the remaining destroyer would be aggressive in its retribution and they didn't have long to wait. The first explosion was perilously close.

The *Ultor* seemed to shudder as some unsecured crockery crashed onto the deck. Several light bulbs flashed off and men tried to appear calm. In quick succession, several other depth charges exploded. The navigation lights on the bridge shattered. The *Ultor* trembled. There still wasn't any serious damage but the intensity and proximity were disturbing. Once again, the crew tried not to show their concern, but kept on with their business, glued to their jobs.

Getting them out of there was almost entirely the skipper's responsibility and his alone. In the control room, there was complete

HMS *Conway*, 1930–1932.

HMS *Conway*, 1931. Bantam XV, unbeaten: George Hunt played twelve matches, won all twelve!

George's first ship, *Arracan*. P. Henderson Line of Glasgow, 1932–34.

HMS *Achilles* – Second Cruiser Squadron, Home Fleet, 1935. Six months' training for George as midshipman.

Midshipman G.E. Hunt RNR, age 18.

Sub Lieutenant G.E. Hunt RNR 1937, age 20.

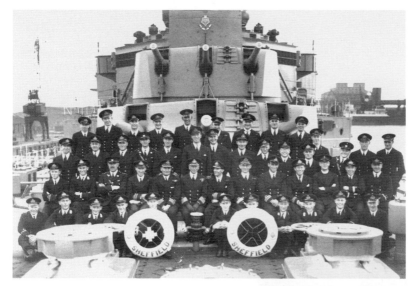

HMS *Sheffield*, Third Cruiser Squadron, Home Fleet, 1937. George trained in her for several months.

George and Phoebe's wedding day, 24 November 1939, in Edinburgh.

This shows the naming of the Polish submarine *Sokol* at Vickers by General Sikorski in December 1940.

Lieutenant George Hunt on his return to the UK from the Mediterranean, ready to take his CO's qualifying course, January 1942.

Petty Officer Phoebe Hunt on leave in Moffat shortly before her promotion to Chief Wren, 1942.

HM Submarine *Proteus*, rammed by Italian destroyer the *Sagittario*.

George's first command, HM Submarine *H50* – training, west coast of Scotland and Northern Ireland.

Con Thode (First Lt), George Hunt (Captain), Michael Carter (3rd Hand) – June to November 1942.

Phoebe launching HM Submarine *Tally Ho*. Cutting the ribbon on her birthday, 23 December 1942, at Vickers Limited, Barrow-in-Furness.

HMS *Ultor* returning from patrol to Malta, flying the Jolly Roger, 1943.

The *Champagne*. The *Ultor* torpedoed her as she came out of the harbour. She is lying here with a broken back, 24 September 1943.

Barry Charles (in picture), Charles Pels and George boarded the *Champagne* after the Germans had left Bastia. The place was a shambles.

La Maddalena, September 1944. HMS *Ultor*'s ship's company and Jolly Roger before their return to the UK.

HM Submarine *Ultor* returning to the UK after two years in the Mediterranean.

HM Submarine *Taku*. George's third command, working out of Blyth, Northumberland, October 1944 to April 1945.

May 1945. George was one of two Submarine Officers who were selected by the Admiralty to have their portraits painted for the Imperial War Museum.

Victory parade through the city of Southampton, June 1946 – Lt Cdr. Hunt leading.

George's fourth sea command, HM Submarine *Ambush*, April 1947.

HMS *Theseus* entering Grand Harbour, Malta, October 1952 (George second in command). A grand sight!

Admiral Lord Louis Mountbatten, C-in-C Mediterranean, coming on board his flagship HMS *Theseus* in Malta, October 1952.

This shows the First Lord of the Admiralty visiting HMS *Theseus* and inspecting the band. George was a member of the RN Pipers' Society.

HMS *Bigbury Bay*, April 1956 – George appointed Senior Naval Officer West Indies with the rank of Commodore.

HMS *Ulster* came to Bermuda to relieve HMS *Bigbury Bay*, and George commanded her for several months.

February 1957. George took *Bigbury Bay* to Havana, Cuba – seen here with the British Ambassador Mr A.S. Fordham and the President, General Fulgencio Batista (Fidel Castro took over three weeks later).

Bermuda, 1957. G.E. Hunt being piped on board HMCS *Algonquin* – returning the call of the senior officers of the Canadian Squadron.

Inauguration of the West Indies Federation by HRH Princess Margaret, Trinidad, April 1958.

Lord Hales, Governor General; Mr Grantley Adams, Prime Minister; HRH; Sir Edward Beetham, Governor of Trinidad; George (in background) and Sir John Francis, Speaker of the House.

HM The Queen giving her colour to the Colour Officer at a ceremony on 8 June, 1959, in recognition of the fiftieth year of submarines in the Royal Navy.

The Queen's colour held by the Submarine Command is paraded officially for the first time after the presentation in the presence of Her Majesty.

George and Phoebe attended the launching of HM Submarine *Dreadnought* by HM The Queen, 21 October, 1960. This was Britain's first nuclear-powered submarine, built by Vickers Limited at Barrow-in-Furness.

silence. George remained calm, gently giving directions to change the course, speed and depth occasionally. During these attacks, he would console himself by thinking how difficult it was in reality for a depth charge to actually hit – it needed to be really close and accurate in three planes; forward, sideways and vertical.

However, when he heard the swish of an enemy ship's propellers increasing with intensity as it passed directly overhead, he involuntarily stiffened. Fortunately there appeared to be only one destroyer doing the attacking, giving George some hope that the other one was at least damaged, and hopefully sunk.

The volatile hammering didn't let up. In all, fifteen depth charges erupted in the most prolonged and fierce attack George had so far experienced in the *Ultor*. (He had of course been subjected to much more when he was First Lieutenant of the *Proteus*, in 1941.)

Eventually, the blasting subsided when the destroyer departed from the area, allowing the *Ultor* to effect a grateful escape.

The next day, on the way back to Malta, George sighted a large enemy supply ship. Unfortunately, as the *Ultor* had fired her full complement of eight torpedoes, he had to allow the vessel to pass unmolested. What a waste.

However, there was plenty of work for the signalman in charge of the Jolly Roger. As well as sewing on a star for the gun action, he would have to stitch on a white bar for the merchant vessel and a red bar for the destroyer. A good patrol's work, George thought.

Back at base, George's pleasure at his success was blunted a little. When reporting the attack, he received a strong rebuke from the Captain of the Tenth Flotilla.

'Hunt. You want to watch it. Firing at destroyers, particularly if there's more than one, may get you in trouble.'

George bit his tongue.

Overall, for the submarine base, the general news was good. The Us had chalked up the most successful month since December 1942. In fact, *Unshaken* had sunk an enemy schooner with the one thousandth torpedo to have been fired in action by a U-class submarine of the Tenth Flotilla.

In the meantime, over the last few weeks, Generals Montgomery and Alexander, and units of the First and Eighth Armies, had arrived in Malta. Thousands of Combined Operation troops and sailors had arrived, as well as tons of equipment and stores, including tanks and invasion barges.

Operation HUSKY was not far off.

CHAPTER TEN

Operation HUSKY

Such are the vagaries of war that Malta, having endured one of history's toughest and longest sieges, was now to be the key base from which the largest invasion of an enemy-held territory in the history of warfare was to be attempted. On 10 July 1943, more than 2,000 naval vessels and landing craft were to carry seven Allied divisions in the assault wave on the largest amphibious operation that had ever been mounted (two more divisions than would land in Normandy less than a year later).

The plans to invade Sicily were extremely detailed. Before an island or territory can be invaded, a prerequisite is to have full details of the beaches where troops would be going ashore and of the enemy defences at these points. The investigations might include surveys of the beaches, acquiring samples of the sand to be assessed as to whether they will tolerate the weight of heavily armed tanks, surveys of beach exits and gun emplacements, and also whether the beaches contain any anti-tank obstacles or mines.

Many of the submarines from the Tenth Flotilla took part in landing some brave souls on these missions. On the actual D-Day, many submarines would be used as 'marker beacons' to ensure the invading force landed on the correct beaches. In all, twenty-six Allied submarines would be involved in Operation HUSKY, including the one Dutch and the two Polish boats. Five submarines were to form an 'iron ring' patrol across the Gulf of Taranto (the gulf sits in the 'arch' of the foot of Italy).

Allied Command received a special alert as aerial reconnaissance had reported two Italian battleships with supporting cruisers and destroyers to be in the area. All submarines involved (including *Ultor*) were obliged to observe torpedo restrictions while Operation HUSKY was in force; no supply ship under 4,000 tons was to be attacked and one salvo had to be conserved for attacks on cruisers and heavier ships.

The *Ultor* left Malta on the evening of 1 July with two other Tenth Flotilla Us, *Sokol* and *Unruly*, to take up positions north of the Straits of Messina. Their orders were to sink any hostile shipping north of Messina, but also to comply with the special torpedo restrictions in force during the operation. The first week was generally uneventful, but as the date of the invasion drew closer, marine activity hotted up.

On the evening of the 8th, George received a signal concerning the presence in the area of a large merchant vessel. Some time after 10.00pm, the *Ultor* was close inshore and charging her batteries on the surface. It was always a relief to surface as submarines were submerged almost constantly during the day and the atmosphere soon became fairly rank, smelling of sweat, diesel fumes and increasingly rancid food. That night was no different.

Outside, the evening was fresh; there was a slight swell and visibility was moderate. Then, at about 1,600 yards out to sea, George noticed the darkened shape of a ship moving briskly across his vision at 14 knots. It was the 8,000-ton merchant vessel *Valfiorita*. He also noted a destroyer escort weaving in the background. The *Valfiorita* would be his next target.

As the ship was moving quite quickly, George decided to fire his first torpedo while the *Ultor* was on the surface, and to fire the rest on the way down. He ordered four torpedoes to be prepared. He quickly calculated he would need a spread of a ship's length and a half, with the point of aim of the first torpedo to be at a quarter length ahead. Information from the plot confirmed the calculations.

At almost 10.45pm, George fired the first torpedo. It shot out of its tube leaving an angry eddy in its wake. He then dived the boat. As she submerged, the next three torpedoes were launched at nine and a half-second intervals.

The *Ultor* had hardly levelled at the bottom of her dive when the crew heard the reflected sound of three clear explosions. The *Valfiorita* had been well and truly hit, but the destroyer escort wasn't going to let them get away lightly. The crew's excitement was brief as they braced themselves for their expected pounding. Sure enough, within a few minutes, depth charges started exploding all around the submarine.

Some came close, causing vibrations and a lot of noise, but most erupted harmlessly in the distance. In all, it was the longest bombardment George had experienced in the *Ultor*. The destroyer was very persistent and dropped thirty depth charges around them. The incident was of concern as George found there was some damage: a leaking stern gland which would certainly require attention quite urgently.

Some time later, George brought the *Ultor* up to periscope depth and, at a safe distance, surveyed the damage he had incurred on the *Valfiorita* through the powerful binocular lenses. The ship was burning furiously, the flames eerily reflecting off the water and highlighting ghostly images of men frantically abandoning her. The destroyer was picking up survivors from the ocean as well as from the lifeboats. George was pleased enough about the men being saved, but, ultimately he could not allow himself to be too concerned about sailors floating in the water. They were in the middle of a very savage war; Britain was fighting for its existence.

The *Valfiorita* was now in her death throes. She would only last a few more minutes. The Navigating Officer had a simple Brownie camera which he held up to the periscope and captured the moment on film.

Later that evening, as the *Ultor* surfaced for recharging, as always George reminded himself to be careful as he slowly eased the clips off the conning tower hatch. After firing four or more torpedoes, the barometer records a very significant air pressure increase inside the submarine. Such is the difference in pressure, an individual can be blown out over the side as the hatch is opened. He was always mindful of the case of the CO of a U-class boat being blown overboard when the boat surfaced and he was lost. When surfacing,

George and most COs made a practice of having the signalman, who usually followed his Captain up the conning tower, hang on to his legs until the upper hatch was fully open and pressure vented.

The next day, 9 July, the day before the landing, the weather had become appalling. Strong north-westerly winds increased to gale force that afternoon. There was a widespread feeling that the invasion would have to be postponed. But the huge fleet of troop transports, store ships, petrol carriers, oilers and landing craft was committed. There was to be no turning back.

George imagined how miserable it would be for the soldiers in the landing craft, many of them already seasick, running on to the open beaches through crashing surf and vicious, raging spray. Also, how difficult it would be for the airborne assault forces – the paratroopers and those attempting to land in gliders.

George was frustrated on the day of the landing, 10 July, and the next day, as three separate German U-boats passed within 1,000 yards of him. Because of the recent torpedo restrictions in force, he could not have a go at them and had to let them pass.

Between them, the three Tenth Squadron submarines in the area, *Ultor, Sokol* and *Unruly*, had sighted no less than ten German U-boats moving through the Straits of Messina in a period of four days. By the time the firing restrictions had been lifted on the 13th, they were only able to sink one. These German U-boats had been sent in response to the invasion of Sicily and were on their way to attack the amphibious forces. The restriction not to attack any U-boats was infuriating to the three submarine COs, especially as they later found out the U-boats went on to sink two British cruisers.

The decision to impose torpedo restrictions came in for considerable criticism. The planners, however, had been only too aware of the real danger of enemy cruisers and battleships attacking the invasion force. Allied torpedoes had to be saved for them.

There was some impatience as the crew were in the dark over the success, or otherwise, of the landings, but on 15 July, they received messages that the invasion was going well. The same day, the *Ultor* was relieved by another U-class submarine, the *Unsparing*. Along with *Sokol* and *Unruly*, the *Ultor* was ordered to make her way to

Bizerta, a port in Tunisia. This was to keep them clear of 'friendly fire' while Allied forces were streaming back and forth from Tunisia, Malta and Sicily. They were ordered to wait there for either an escort or a convoy to take them back to Malta.

There was some satisfaction while in Bizerta, where they noted the spoils of war left by the defeated Afrika Korps. The area was littered with burnt-out panzers, trucks and equipment, vestiges of their last stand.

The three submarines stayed in Bizerta until 24 July. At this stage, the convoy and assault lines were much less crowded. *Sokol* and *Unruly* were then escorted back to Malta, while *Ultor* was escorted to Algiers. Here George reported to the Special Operations Executive (SOE) where he was given some munitions in drums – these and other items of war were to be handed over to some Italian Resistance railway workers on his next patrol. George and his Navigating Officer, Charlie Pels, were very carefully briefed regarding the exact location of their contact with the Italian Resistance.

By this time, the assault phase of HUSKY was complete. The seaborne landings had produced remarkably few casualties and by now invading Allied troops were busily mopping up resistance across Sicily.

The Allies would soon be able to turn their attention to invading the Italian mainland.

CHAPTER ELEVEN

Operation AVALANCHE

The war was not going well for the Italians. On 25 July 1943, the Fascist dictator, Benito Mussolini, who had ruled Italy with an iron fist for over twenty years, was finally overthrown, to be replaced by Marshal Badoglio. Events moved fast. By early August, the Marshal was putting out clandestine peace feelers. As the negotiations continued throughout the month, carefully concealed from the Germans, the Allies decided to land on mainland Italy as soon as possible.

The original plan was to land at Crotone in the Gulf of Taranto, but this was changed to an amphibious crossing of the Straits of Messina followed by a landing at Salerno, 80 kilometres south of Naples on the west coast. This was Operation AVALANCHE and it was scheduled for the first week of September.

Except for a couple of submarines needed to act as beacon markers on the actual day, submarines were not considered necessary for the Allied crossing of the Straits. Most of the Tenth Flotilla submarines therefore continued with hunting enemy shipping around the Mediterranean.

During the invasion of Sicily, warships of the Italian fleet had been reported in the Gulf of Taranto and it was known they were still there. A plan was produced to sink the two large battleships, *Doria* and *Duilio*, as a means of keeping them from assisting the defence of Salerno. Known as Operation BOTTOM, it would involve the *Ultor* and *Unrivalled*, another Tenth Flotilla submarine. These two boats would each transport a manned explosives weapon, a 'chariot', to the enemy harbour, following which the *Ultor* was to carry out a dummy beach reconnaissance. George was also to drop pieces of naval equipment on a beach at Crotone in an effort to deceive the enemy that an invasion was imminent in the area. Then, at the request of the SOE, he would proceed to a rendezvous on the Italian Adriatic coast and deliver some munitions in sealed drums, which had been delivered to him from Algiers, to a group of disaffected Italian railway workers. These men would carry out acts of sabotage as much as they could to disrupt the Germans and help to hasten the end of the war in Italy.

The chariots had been developed after an intrepid team of Italian frogmen had damaged two British battleships, *Valiant* and *Queen Elizabeth*, in December 1941 in Alexandria harbour. Each two-man chariot was 25 feet long with an explosive charge of up to 700lb carried in the bow; the charge could be detached and slung beneath the target ship. Battery powered, the chariot had a top speed of 5 knots, but a range of only 20 miles (35 kilometres) so would have to be transported on specially adapted submarines to well within that distance of the target. The crew sat astride the torpedo, behind protective shields, wearing special breathing apparatus that left no bubbles.

A number of similar chariots had been used by the Italians in operations before at Malta and Alexandria, sometimes with tragic consequences for their brave crewmen. For this attack, the four British 'charioteers' spent most of the month practising, making three dummy attacks on the battleship *Rodney* in the Grand Harbour at Valletta, each time succeeding in penetrating the defensive nets.

When the *Ultor* and *Unrivalled* sailed from Malta on 24 August, with the chariots attached 'bare back', as it was called, everyone was confident of success. (To carry the chariots, wooden chocks were attached to the after casing of the submarine behind the conning tower.)

Two days later, the boats reached the heavily-guarded Italian naval base of Taranto. Just as the charioteers were preparing for their mission, the submarine COs received disappointing news when they were ordered to cancel the attack by the chariots. No reason was given, which did not help to console the depressed charioteers. The fact was that the secret negotiations with the Italians convinced the Allies that the Italian battle fleet would surrender on the same day as the landings at Salerno on 9 September. There was no point in destroying the battleships, which might be used by the Allies. *Unrivalled* was ordered to return to Malta but the *Ultor* was to continue (on her second mission of this patrol) with the plan to make the enemy believe that a landing would still take place in the Crotone area.

As George proceeded south towards Crotone, in the early morning of the 28th, as they passed Punta Alice (Point Alice), he saw an Italian warship, a 680-ton destroyer – or a torpedo boat – the *Lince*. The vessel had gone aground on the sand and shingle beach. He noticed that it wasn't damaged – the bow was aground and the stern was afloat – and realized that the Captain had simply 'cut the corner' too close to the beach. Salvage workers were trying desperately to refloat her; she was a sitting duck. The ship, in fact, had been there since 17 August when the *United*, another of the Tenth Flotilla Us, had earlier spotted her, but it was the *United*'s final Mediterranean patrol and the Captain assumed there were mines somewhere between his boat and the target. However, because of superstition that tragedy could strike his last patrol, he decided not to attack the *Lince* and continued on his way.

Ten days later, the *United*, returning from her mission, found the destroyer still aground. The *United* was in 75 fathoms and the Captain would have liked to approach to 50 fathoms. This would increase his chances of success, but once again he was simply not prepared to take that risk on his way back from his last patrol.

George, however, did not hesitate. Undeterred by rumours of minefields and using his Asdic, 'pinging' in active mode, he carefully approached the beach and was able to get reasonably close to the stranded vessel, which had a tug and another smallish vessel in attendance. An army of toiling Italians and a bulldozer were working on the beach, digging a channel in order to free the ship. George noticed some gunners standing at action stations by the ship's guns.

The morning sun was still low and visibility was good. There was, however, a strongish tide running which was of concern. George didn't want to take the risk that the current would deflect his torpedo. He therefore took his time and circled around twice until he had the enemy vessel set up perfectly. He would allow himself one torpedo.

While at periscope depth, George took the boat in to 900 yards and ordered one torpedo to be prepared. He took a quick photograph of the stricken vessel through the periscope then, just before 8.15am, the torpedo was released and raced towards the destroyer. It smashed in exactly where it was aimed – just under the mainmast. There was a resounding crash and George told the crew that the ship had broken its back. Sea water raced into the gaping crack causing the stern to fall away quickly and sink. The vessel would be going nowhere.

'We've just saved the Italians from a hot day's work in the sun,' George joked. However, the action wasn't over. The gun crew on the forepart of the destroyer, which remained afloat, manned the last surviving gun, turned it and fired an angry fusillade at the *Ultor*'s periscope. Fortunately, the shells went wide. Admiring their spirit, George took another quick photograph before turning to head out to sea.

Ultor then continued on with her second mission: to plant 'evidence' of an impending invasion around Crotone and other beaches. In an effort to deceive the enemy, George had been given orders to approach the beach and deposit his 'props'. This was not a foolhardy request to proceed in so close as the question of mines had been discussed with the staff before he sailed, but it was considered that mines were not a threat due to the depth of the water.

That night, *Ultor* surfaced just offshore and George launched two folbots, (collapsible two-man canoes, capable of being manipulated through the torpedo loading hatch), a buoy and other incriminating equipment. For good measure, he jettisoned a sailor's cap. An onshore breeze did the rest. While reporting the incident in the log, at the bottom of the page he drew a pirate's sword indicating the status of the mission.

Having disposed of the *Lince* and then carried out the deception of an impending invasion in the area, George took the *Ultor* across the Gulf and then up the east coast of Italy to a secluded bay in the vicinity of Barletta, where he was to deliver the dozen drums of munitions given to him by the SOE in Algiers.

The signalman flashed a recognition signal towards the shore and waited. The signals were the letters K and R in Morse code – dash-dot-dash followed by dot-dash-dot. In due course, a rowing boat stealthily approached from the bay. The rower called out, 'Fondo alla pasta.'

To which George replied, 'Saint Angelo.'

Satisfied he had made the right connection, George invited the man on board. His name was Joseph and George offered him a cigarette. The drums, already tied to each other by short lengths of rope, were to be laid in a line in the water. They would later be caught by a grapnel towed behind a boat. George pointed out to Joseph the position where they would be laid.

The contents of the drums consisted of rifles, pistols, ammunition, plastic explosives – and land mines cunningly made to look like horse droppings and chunks of mud. These unassuming surprises could simply be laid on roads, ready to be run over by vehicles. As George was returning Joseph to his boat, another boat arrived bearing gifts of fish. The occupants were given a bottle of whisky. With those tasks completed, *Ultor* started back towards Malta.

On the return journey, while sailing past Point Alice where the *Lince* had been destroyed, George noted the result of his torpedo with some satisfaction. There were still casualties being tended in makeshift shelters on the beach and no doubt some men in the destroyer would have gone down with the after part.

George had little in the way of sensitive emotions towards this loss of life. Compassion for the enemy was still a long way away – this was simply total war. He still had strong feelings of indignation at Germany's barbaric attacks on Britain right from the beginning of the war. At the same time, he felt some satisfaction at destroying an enemy vessel that had been specifically designed and built for sinking submarines. The war would be that much closer to being finished. Meanwhile, he was only too thankful to be on his way back to base. The last two or three days had been packed with action and interest, but very little sleep.

During August, submarines from the three Flotillas had had a good month. Their aggression was paying off as, collectively, they had sunk two warships, the *Gioberti* and the *Lince*, and eight other merchant vessels.

On 3 September 1943, the Eighth Army crossed the Straits of Messina and landed on the mainland with little opposition. They then advanced rapidly up the 'toe' of Italy, with the intention of eventually meeting up with the Salerno landing force.

That same day, an armistice with the Italians was agreed, including the 'arrangement' that Italy would become the Allies' 'co-belligerents'. However, it was considered necessary to withhold the news of the surrender until the evening of 8 September, the day before AVALANCHE, the main landings at Salerno. With most of the Italian fleet at La Spezia, in northern Italy, the Allied Commander-in-Chief, Admiral Cunningham, gave the order for the Italian fleet to sail to Malta and formally surrender at 3.00pm on 9 September, half an hour before the Salerno landings were to begin.

Meanwhile, the landings at Salerno continued as planned, with 500 naval vessels taking part. With the news of Italy's surrender only a few hours earlier, the Italians had vacated their positions, most of them leaving their weapons behind and heading for home. The war, they felt, was over for them.

The Germans, however, were another matter and the invasion was opposed by well-prepared German defences. At the end of the first day, the British and Americans had established a beachhead, but they were meeting stiff resistance. Two days later, the invasion had bogged down to a battle of attrition.

That same day, the 11th, the Italian fleet from La Spezia was led in to Malta by Admiral Cunningham's flagship, the battleship HMS *Warspite*. Here they were met by an assembly of nine Allied warships, including one Greek and one French ship.

For all in the harbour, especially George, this was a marvellous sight to see.

George and his First Lieutenant, Barry Rowe, had borrowed a dinghy and sailed out beyond the harbour. This way they were able to gain 'ringside seats' to witness the Italian fleet arrive and anchor. The Italian fleet consisted of fifteen warships, including two battleships, five cruisers, seven destroyers and torpedo boats. They were soon

91

joined by other remnants of the Italian fleet: four warships from Genoa, five from Taranto, one from Paola and three from other Adriatic ports.

To George, it was one of the most memorable days of the war. Here were the enemy warships, whose silhouettes he knew by heart – the very ones he had been hunting and dreaming of sinking. Now they were meekly being led to an anchorage off Grand Harbour and suffering the humiliation of having their flags hauled down. It was an historic occasion, one that was imprinted in George's memory. The victory to the Allies was complete when, two days later, on 13 September, Admiral Cunningham sent an historic signal to all ships: 'I have this day informed the Board of Admiralty that the Italian fleet now lies at anchor under the guns of the fortress of Malta.'

CHAPTER TWELVE

Champagne

The landings at Salerno and the surrender of the Italian Fleet immediately changed the focus of operations for the Tenth Flotilla. The Commander-in-Chief ordered all submarines in the Flotilla not to sail until further orders and by 14 September 1943, all boats except *Sokol* were in harbour. (*Sokol* was on a mission to Brindisi on Italy's east coast to persuade the Italians there to surrender.)

The few days' break gave George an opportunity to stroll around Malta and see the sights. As he made his way through the rubble and devastation which crowded the narrow side streets, alleyways and piazzas of Valletta, he marvelled at how anybody had survived. Some of the buildings were centuries old and, amazingly, a few were still standing, including the medieval cathedral of St John, a legacy of Crusader days.

It also gave George time to catch up on mail from home. While in the Mediterranean, he received correspondence once a month, often with two or three letters in the bundle from Phoebe. George would write in turn on a postcard-size letter called an aerograph, which was made of very thin paper and allowed space for a very brief message. Home mail was always welcome – it gave the fighting men a clear and real reminder of why they were there.

The break from hostilities also allowed time to relax on the large balcony at Lazaretto. The protective walls were about 40 centimetres thick and comfortable chairs allowed those relaxing to enjoy a commanding view of the harbour from the wide verandahs. The war, however, was still never far away and the break didn't last for long.

As most of the S-class and T-class submarines were now being sent to join the fight in the Pacific, it was decided that the U-class boats, with their lesser endurance capacity, should be relocated closer to the action. A team was sent to reconnoitre La Maddalena, an island which was once a major Italian naval base on the north-eastern tip of Sardinia (by coincidence, it had also been the home of the Italian Tenth Submarine Flotilla). Sardinia, and its neighbour Corsica, were large islands off the west coast of Italy in the Tyrrhenian Sea. The German garrison had recently abandoned Sardinia and were in the process of escaping across the Strait of Bonifacio to Corsica, and then to the Italian mainland.

Meanwhile, on the mainland at Salerno, the Allied invasion force had run into serious trouble. However, on the 16th, Montgomery completed his charge up from the 'toe' and the two armies linked up. Now they could begin the hard slog north.

George's next patrol involved preventing German troops from evacuating Corsica and meeting up with the German Army on the Italian mainland. Even now they were congregating in the north of Corsica awaiting transport. The only four available Us were *Ultor*, *Unseen*, *Uproar* and the Polish boat *Dzik*. They left just after nightfall on the 15th and, with the security of an escort through the narrows, made their way to Bastia, a coastal town on the north-east coast of Corsica, the point where the Germans were being evacuated by air and sea.

George patrolled the seas north and east of Corsica for several days and then moved closer to the harbour at Bastia. On 22 September, he sighted a huge tanker, the largest he had seen – 9,945 tons – berthed at the wharf inside the harbour. It was the *Champagne*. Other Us had attacked it before, but had failed to sink her. There was a low breakwater in the harbour and the ship was sitting high in the water. George could clearly see that she was taking on board large quantities of supplies and army equipment, particularly lorries and field guns. When the Germans had vacated North Africa, they moved a certain amount of their supplies and men to Corsica and were now reloading it to be added to their war effort on the mainland.

George noted there were six escorts patrolling around the bay: two corvettes and four E-boats. He realized his only chance of sinking the tanker was to torpedo her just as she came out of the harbour. It would also be better value then as she would be fully laden. He decided he would sit it out – he would watch her for as long as it took.

For the next three days, George patiently monitored the vessel, moving around outside the harbour at periscope depth, keeping note of the loading process. At night, the *Ultor* would return to the open sea to recharge her batteries, but the OOW would always keep an eye on the harbour entrance.

George continued with this strategy until he was interrupted in the early hours of the morning of the 24th. While the *Ultor* was charging batteries on the surface, he sighted another large marine tanker, proceeding at 12 knots between him and the coast. He also noted that the vessel was escorted by two destroyers. As it was still dark, George, on the bridge, brought the *Ultor* to within 1,400 yards, having used radar to check the range of his target. With the benefits of the 'fruit machine' (a calculator-type piece of equipment below in the control room), his Navigating Officer calculated the enemy course, track angle and other data for the torpedoes.

George ordered four torpedoes to be brought to the ready. Visibility was poor and the target was set against the darkened backdrop of the land mass. It was always going to be a difficult shot as the vessel's silhouette was almost lost. George aimed the first torpedo just ahead of the bow.

At 3.49am, he fired the first torpedo. To George and the crew's annoyance, the first two torpedoes missed the tanker and continued on towards the shore, which unfortunately alerted the enemy vessels. The tanker turned her guns on the *Ultor* and the destroyers gave chase. Both destroyers then opened fire on the *Ultor*, which was still on the surface.

George abandoned the firing of the last two torpedoes. Shells whistled past the submarine, some hitting the water close by and landing with a resounding crash. Water spouts splashed 20 feet high, the moonlight catching the frothy fall-out as it cascaded into the ocean. George moved quickly to the conning tower hatch and pressed the klaxon. He briskly shut and clipped the hatch behind him, then clattered down the ladder, rapping out the orders, 'Take her down to 200 feet, shut off for depth-charge attack and go to silent routine.' He continued with directions to the Navigating Officer, 'Bring her round to 180 degrees and go slow ahead, both motors, group down.'

The *Ultor* dived and the crew waited for the expected depth charges.

After an indeterminate amount of time and a degree of tension, no depth charges were dropped. With relief, George took the *Ultor* stealthily out of the area and manoeuvred back to a position where he could observe Bastia harbour and his initial intended prey. As dawn broke on the 24th, with the excitement of the early morning's action behind them, the crew of the *Ultor* settled in once again, the boat back at periscope depth. George continued to bide his time as he observed the Germans loading the tanker.

The loading of the *Champagne* continued all day with guns, lorries, ammunition and all types of equipment needed to run an army stowed on board. Late in the afternoon, George noticed a wisp of smoke blowing out of her funnel. They had lit the boilers.

'They're raising steam,' he called. 'It won't be long now. We'll get ready. Bring all four tubes to the action state.'

Water flooded into the tubes surrounding the torpedoes.

Just on twilight, the *Champagne*, assisted by tugs, left her berth and, moving slowly, headed out of the harbour into a calm sea. Every precaution against attack had been made. Her six escorts, four of which preceded the tanker, formed a formidable screen around her. As they chaperoned her out of the harbour entrance, the two corvettes and four E-boats were disposed one ahead and one astern and two either side. This increased the challenge to George, but served only to whet his appetite.

He painted a 'word picture' of the situation 'up top' for the benefit of the crew. George liked to keep everyone informed and it kept them all interested and 'on their toes'. Then, moving cautiously, he manoeuvred the *Ultor* under one of the corvettes and finished up inside the screen. He worked into a position inside the port bow of one of the corvettes. He was in dangerous territory but he was now less than 1,800 yards from his target; it was close enough.

Less than ten minutes after the *Champagne* had left the harbour, George was in position and ready. They were now in nearly 25 fathoms of water which would give him room to go deep and escape. At two minutes before 8.00pm, George fired the first torpedo. After firing the second torpedo he told the First Lieutenant, 'Take her down to 100 feet and shut off for depth-charging.'

Seventy seconds later, the first of the torpedoes smashed into the *Champagne*. Twelve seconds later, the crew of the *Ultor* heard the second one crash into it also.

The Captain of the *Champagne* reacted quickly. He turned the vessel hard to starboard and aimed for the security of the land. The tanker bolted blindly through the semi-darkness and a few minutes later, hit the beach. A sickening grinding sound echoed into the night as the *Champagne* broke her back. For George and his crew there was hardly time for celebration as the escorts raced towards the *Ultor*.

Within minutes, the first depth charge exploded nearby and shook the submarine. The crew braced themselves and withstood seven more blasts all very close. Once again, the *Ultor* emerged shaken but unharmed and George spirited her away from the area.

Next morning at 8.00, George took the *Ultor* back into Bastia Bay. While searching for signs of his success of the previous evening, he found the *Champagne* beached less than half a kilometre south of Bastia. She was simply sitting on the 'putty' (sand and mud), where she had beached herself. It looked like she had suffered serious damage and wouldn't be going anywhere; periscope photographs clearly showed later that she had broken her back.

At the same time that George had sighted the beached tanker, he sighted through the periscope a 100-ton Siebel ferry. These ships were fast, well-armed landing craft and were valid targets. However, the vessel was escorted by four anti-submarine trawlers. Even though they were small, they carried a sting in their tail, with guns and depth charges.

George planned to use his last two torpedoes. He would fire one at the ferry and give a parting shot to the *Champagne*. He was 1,000 yards from the ferry, which was stopped, and 2,000 yards from the *Champagne*.

The bay was calm and visibility good. At 9.45am George fired the first torpedo at the Siebel ferry and the second one at the *Champagne*, aimed just below the bridge. The first explosion echoed back to the crew just over a minute later. It was a direct hit on the ferry which quickly began to sink.

Two minutes after firing, another explosion was heard coming from the vicinity of the *Champagne*. George couldn't make out if the torpedo had actually struck the vessel or the rocks behind. Meanwhile, he went deep as the four escorts gave chase. Only one appeared to have depth charges and over the next few minutes created havoc in the quiet waters of the bay. In all, twelve explosions crashed all around.

For the second time in two days, the crew of the *Ultor* weathered the pummelling. Some were quite close, buffeting the submarine, but incurring no real damage. Once again, luck was on their side.

As they had fired their last torpedo, George moved away from the scene and returned the *Ultor* to Malta.

In the meantime, the other three Us on the same mission had achieved similar successes. On 21 September, *Dzik* sank the 6,397-ton German supply ship *Nicolauo Ourania* (formerly Greek) at the entrance to Bastia harbour. The following day she sank three Siebel ferries.

Unseen achieved a remarkable result off La Spezia on 21 September by putting a torpedo into two enemy ships in one salvo. *Brandenburg*, the 3,894-ton auxiliary minesweeper and *Kreta* (2,600 tons) went to the bottom together.

The fourth submarine of the group, *Uproar*, achieved another remarkable result the following day. While off the island of Elba, she hit the *Andre Sgarallino*, a 731-ton naval auxiliary with three torpedoes out of three fired. To finish off the patrol, on 27 September, *Uproar*, while passing the beached tanker *Champagne*, fired a single torpedo into her stern.

So ended this climactic month for the Fighting Tenth, as the Flotilla had been named. The Italians had surrendered, Allied forces were now well and truly established on mainland Italy and the enemy were inexorably retreating. The Tenth had left Lazaretto and Malta and was soon to be based at their new home in Algiers.

The final phase was about to begin.

CHAPTER THIRTEEN

French Riviera

The official assessment of the role of the submarines in the Mediterranean after the Italian armistice was that their main work was completed. Targets were restricted to only German and German-controlled shipping in diminished operational areas. Most of the large ships had been sunk and German shipbuilders were unable to make up for such losses. However, the Germans had recovered their grip on the Greek Islands and many of the submarines were sent to operate in the Aegean.

At the end of September 1943, there were twenty-eight Allied operational submarines in the Mediterranean. La Maddalena had been heavily bombed by the US Air Force and was still not ready for use. As the Tenth Flotilla at Malta was too distant from the action, the majority of submarine patrols in October were made from the depot ship *Maidstone* at Algiers, headquarters of the Eighth Submarine Flotilla. This is where *Ultor* was at the beginning of October 1943.

Several submarines, *Dolfijn*, a Dutch boat, *Unseen* and *Ultor*, were ordered to patrol the seas around the French Riviera and the Gulf of Genoa. The *Ultor* left Algiers on 11 October bound for the Gulf. One of her aims was to try to sink German U-boats which were known to be based at La Spezia in Italy and Toulon on the Riviera.

The *Ultor* searched uneventfully for a week, then, late on the morning of the 19th, in an area north-west of La Spezia, near Civitavecchia, George sighted a 3,500-ton German passenger ship, the *Aversa*. The vessel had been formerly owned by the Greeks and was known then as the *Kakoulima*. The Germans were now using it to transport troops and military cargo. The sky was overcast and light rain was falling, interfering with visibility and to George's annoyance, the moisture kept fogging up the periscope. However, he could clearly see four escorts: a corvette, an E-boat and two anti-submarine schooners.

The *Aversa* was travelling north at 10 knots and even though there was a stiff sou'-sou'-easterly blowing, she was a steady target.

George ordered the Torpedo Officer to bring four torpedoes to the ready. He took the *Ultor* in to 2,200 yards range and aimed the first torpedo half a length ahead of the *Aversa*. Calculating a spread of two ships' lengths, he fired the first of the four torpedoes at 11.41am. The remaining torpedoes raced towards the target fourteen seconds apart.

Immediately the *Ultor* planed down to 200 feet while the crew waited for a result. One minute and fifty-five seconds later, they were rewarded when one torpedo was heard to hit the vessel. Twenty-five seconds later a second one smashed into the target. Another white bar would be added to their Jolly Roger. After a round of cheers, they braced themselves for the customary drubbing. However, twenty minutes later, none was forthcoming; the enemy had not dropped any depth charges. George cautiously took the *Ultor* back to periscope depth and was delighted to witness the *Aversa* finally sinking – a compelling scene.

Dinghies and lifeboats were floating around the damaged vessel and stricken sailors were being pulled out of the sea by the escorts. The moment was urgent. Water was racing into the holds of the *Aversa* and she was sinking fast. At exactly one minute past noon, the passenger vessel sat upright, majestically waving her bows in the air. She hovered there for a few seconds, tottered, and then gravity took over. She plummeted straight down, stern first, to be drawn under the dark, stormy waters. The ocean and the war would claim another offering.

Next morning, George moved north towards Genoa. At sunrise, the weather had cleared into a beautiful day. The water was glassy calm and, at periscope depth, George commanded a clear view of the harbour entrance. To his excitement, coming out of the harbour at 8 knots was a 3,000-ton cargo ship. The vessel was known as a KT ship – *Kriegstransporter* – many of which were mass-produced as merchant carriers. She was accompanied by a destroyer and two E-boats.

Initially, he was concerned that the fine day and glassy water conditions might work against him. If the lookouts of any of the four vessels were alert, it would be possible to sight the tracks of the torpedoes, as had happened to him previously.

George realized that if the Captain of the enemy ship did sight the torpedoes, the chances of him diverting his ship were minimal. Although it would increase his own vulnerability, the target was too good to pass up. It was worth a risk.

George took the *Ultor* in to 1,800 yards range and ordered four torpedoes to be brought to the ready. He planned to spread the four torpedoes over a length and a half. That way, he hoped at least one would hit the bow, midships or stern. At 7.26, he started firing the torpedoes at thirteen-second intervals.

Because of the risk of being detected, George told the First Lieutenant to go to 200 feet, shut off for depth-charge attack and go to silent routine. As they levelled out at 200 feet, the crew listened intently for the expected sound of the torpedoes' impact. Unfortunately, after three minutes, a reasonable amount of time for the torpedoes to hit, to everyone's disappointment, there was no response. A minute later, the torpedoes slammed into the beach over 5,000 yards away. They had clearly missed the ship.

Then the depth charges started to crash around them extremely accurately.

'Damn,' said George. 'I'm sure they saw the torpedoes coming. They must have combed the tracks.' The crew braced themselves.

Once again, lights flashed off. Equipment and some unsecured articles crashed down. The boat shook violently. Men grasped whatever they could for stability.

In all, nine depth charges were dropped on them. It was the most precise and intense attack that George had encountered. This time, the *Ultor* wasn't so lucky – she had suffered some damage, including a badly leaking stern gland, but she was still serviceable. It was a stressful few moments, but the experience would serve to harden the crew – there would be tougher times ahead, but *Ultor* had been very lucky.

The other two submarines in the area, *Dolfijn* and *Unseen*, had less excitement than *Ultor*. *Dolfijn* had a largely uneventful mission and *Unseen* sank an F-lighter (another type of anti-submarine trawler). As the three submarines needed repairs or maintenance after the mission, they all returned to Malta.

In the meantime, on 21 October, nine Us were loaned to reinforce the First Flotilla in Beirut, who were engaged in the Aegean. It would appear the Germans were going to make a last stand there – in the Aegean.

The *Ultor* spent most of November at Malta undergoing necessary repairs and maintenance. Once again, for George and the crew, it was a time for catching up on personal administration, mail and recreation.

Meanwhile, in the Aegean, November saw the enemy fighting a bitter and seemingly pointless struggle. Both armies were taking heavy casualties, but by the end of November, the Germans withdrew from the Aegean. At the same time the battle for mainland Italy was still one of desperate attrition.

For the submarines, Operational Command of the western Mediterranean moved officially to La Maddalena, northern Sardinia, which would be ready for action in December. It was decided that the Tenth Flotilla would be maintained at three to five boats and that the new base would bring the name HMS *Talbot* with them from Malta. Even though repairs to the seriously damaged dockyard and accommodation quarters were not finished, it was decided the five core submarines would report there after their next patrol.

The five submarines, *Ultor, Uproar, Untiring, Unseen* and *Universal*, left Malta in late November and early December with instructions to patrol around the French Riviera beaches and La Spezia in northern Italy. George and the *Ultor* left Malta on 7 December to patrol around Toulon on the French Riviera.

Frustratingly, for the first ten days they found nothing except anti-submarine craft. Then, while at periscope depth in the mid-afternoon of the 18th, just off Toulon, George sighted a 250-ton transport barge. This was another Siebel ferry and, being smaller, it only just deserved a torpedo. The option would have been to surface and attack it with the gun. However, as the enemy vessel had more powerful guns, George could not take the risk of the *Ultor* being damaged and perhaps being unable to dive. He would fire two torpedoes at it.

He took the boat in to a range of 1,000 yards. The visibility was good with the sea calm and the weather fine. Just before 3.30 in the afternoon, he fired the first torpedo at the ship's stern and the second almost amidships.

George monitored the scene through the periscope. Fifty seconds later, he watched as the first torpedo smashed into the vessel with spectacular results. On impact, the ship disintegrated, engulfed by a fierce fireball, the innate force shredding the vessel into fragments. The explosion radiated a blinding yellow and red flash. Seconds later, the blast reached George as a resounding 'crump'. By the time the debris had fallen and splashed over the troubled waters, the ship had been swallowed by the ocean. He couldn't make out if the second torpedo had also hit.

In the meantime, the other four Us had encountered varying degrees of success. *Uproar*, while off St Tropez, succeeded in damaging the 11,718-ton Italian liner *Vergilis*, which later sank in the harbour. After her mission, *Uproar* was the first submarine to arrive at the new base at Maddalena on 13 December. *Untiring* followed a German minelayer which went into Monaco Harbour. Cannily, she fired a torpedo through the harbour entrance which hit and exploded the enemy vessel, smashing hundreds of windows in the Principality. A few days later, she sank two coasters.

Unseen didn't encounter any enemy vessels, but five depth charges were accurately dropped on her by an aircraft, causing minor damage. *Universal* sank a steamer, *La Foce*, and sustained a vicious 45-depth-charge reprisal.

Towards the end of December, all Us were safely based at Maddalena, although *Uproar* left again for another patrol on the 24th. Maddalena wasn't a particularly attractive or efficient facility and evoked many unsavoury comments from all who were based there. The Italians had left it in a filthy state. No fresh vegetables or fruit were grown locally so the crews lived mainly on stewed beef. It even lacked decent Italian wine. George noted that docking, repair facilities and spares were limited. He realized that without having Malta under their lee, they would be strongly handicapped in their continued operational successes.

Nonetheless, the end of 1943 saw the Allies still in a strong position, enough to allow a number of submarines to be moved to other 'hot' areas. There were now fifteen submarines operating in the Mediterranean: five at Maddalena and ten from the First Flotilla at Beirut.

Also based at Maddalena was a group of eight American PT boats. These small, fast, well-armed vessels spent most of their time carrying out attacks on enemy coastal traffic, often working with the British Motor Torpedo Boats (MTBs). Friendships soon developed between the crews of the submarines and the PT boats and the American Padre with the PT boats invited the submariners to join them in a Christmas service. The invitation was very welcome as the Tenth Flotilla Padre was still in Malta.

On Christmas day, George was impressed that the Americans had rigged up a huge tent, which soon became full of sailors from both navies, the men sitting on chairs, boxes and stools and enjoying each others' company. The Padre entered, carrying what looked like a suitcase. With some pantomime, he pressed a few buttons and it sprang open to reveal a small harmonium – a type of organ – powered by foot-operated bellows.

The Padre then welcomed everybody by saying, 'Stand, men. The first hymn will be "Onward Christian Soldiers". Youse all know the toon. Now, let 'er go!'

On 26 December, Generals Eisenhower and Montgomery left this theatre of war to plan Operation OVERLORD – the landings in France. Behind them, Allied troops and Germans were bogged down in the mud of a bitter Italian winter, gripped in interminable bloody fighting in the mountains of central Italy. The deadlock would not be eased until the next month, January 1944, when Operation SHINGLE, the Anzio landing south of Rome, took place, in which George and the *Ultor* would be very involved.

CHAPTER FOURTEEN

Operation SHINGLE

At the beginning of 1944, with the exception of a few well-defined areas, the Allies were firmly in control of the Mediterranean. U-boats were always a danger, and there was still a modicum of merchant vessels to sink. However, the *Ultor*'s next mission, George's first from La Maddalena, was to take part in Operation SHINGLE, the Allied landings at Anzio.

Anzio is about 60 kilometres south of Rome. The landing was intended initially to relieve the Allied forces stalled on the Cassino front, about 100 kilometres inland. After that would be the liberation of Rome. Submarines would be needed as beach markers and mine detectors off Anzio – *Ultor* and *Uproar* were the only two boats available at Maddalena. On 13 January, George's orders were to sail for Naples from where they would be given their role for the landings.

Ultor arrived at Naples early in the morning of the 14th and George found that they had a 'day off' before their briefing, which provided an excellent opportunity to do some spontaneous sightseeing. George arranged for some transport and, with eight of his officers and men, set out to visit the ruins of Pompeii, the ancient city buried by the eruptions of Mount Vesuvius in AD 79. Even though George had, by now, visited many sites of antiquity, he was fascinated by the experience. It was a rare treat.

From Naples, the commanding officers of both submarines, together with their Navigating Officers, were transported to Caserta, a town situated on an escarpment about 35 kilometres north-west of

Naples. Here, in a room set up as the Allied Headquarters, they were briefed for the Anzio landings.

The invasion force, as were the armies already pushing north on the mainland, was to be composed of both British and US troops – 40,000 men in all, plus thousands of tanks, trucks and other vehicles of war. The beaches adjacent to Anzio had already been investigated by intrepid reconnaissance parties, so *Ultor* and *Uproar*'s main function would be to mark the beaches that had already been surveyed. *Ultor* was to mark the beach for Force P, carrying the British 1st Division, and *Uproar* was to mark the beach for Force X, the 3rd US Division. Their principal duty was to go in four days beforehand and search for mines with the mine detection units of their Asdic sets, as well as watching the beaches for any untoward activity. They would then act as a beacon to draw the amphibious forces into the correct beach.

The two submarines left Naples after the briefing and moved to a position off the beaches of Anzio. This was dangerous enough as they were now 75 miles behind enemy lines. For the next few days, the two submarines patrolled up and down the beaches, about 1,000 metres offshore.

The exercise proved fruitful, if somewhat nerve-racking. During the first day, to George's satisfaction, they found a minefield, information that would be reported to the minesweepers on the day of the invasion. These vessels would be at the forefront of the landing ships and would then set about sweeping a channel. George was confident that the beaches weren't mined – through the periscope, he had watched German soldiers playing soccer on them.

On the evening of the 21st, the night before the landings, after consultation with Charlie Pels, his Navigator, George positioned the *Ultor* 500 metres off the beach and lined up right in the centre of where the British invasion forces would land. From there, George could see the Anzio lighthouse from which he took bearings. He then dived *Ultor* and rested on the bottom. There they would wait until one hour from H-Hour – 2.00am. At the same time, *Uproar* was marking the beach on the other side of Anzio where the Americans would land.

It was a nervous wait and a long night. The crew realized that next day they could be in the middle of a vicious shooting war – a very heated battle. During the invasion, they had been ordered not to fire a shot, lest they hit their own men on the beaches – to do nothing, just wait. They were also ordered not to move until after the initial landing when an escort would come for them. (George was comfortable with this; he had memories of *Unity* moving in UK home waters, the North Sea, without an escort.)

At 1.00am, George surfaced the *Ultor*, trimmed the boat down very low in the water and anchored. Everything appeared peaceful. To allow the *Ultor* to effect a quick getaway if necessary, he ordered the Second Coxswain to go and sit forward on the fo'c'sle. He supplied him with a life-jacket, a whistle, a torch and a hammer. He told him, 'Break the cable and ride to the anchor on the slip. If something untoward happens such as if a posse of E-boats comes along, your job is to knock off the slip and come quickly back. You should easily be able to get back up and into the bridge before we dive. If you can't, you will have to swim for it, so good luck to you.'

It was a tough call, but all the team were well trained and prepared for this type of situation. George wasn't overly concerned as he realized the man should easily get back to the bridge in time.

He then switched on an infra-red beacon which began flashing out to sea on a certain bearing. This would be the beacon for the Allied invasion force to home in on. George was mindful of the importance of this role – his father had landed at Cape Helles in the First World War at Gallipoli in 1915. Every military commander since then had been aware that the naval midshipmen, during that landing on an unmarked beach, dropped the ANZAC troops at the wrong location, with disastrous consequences. George, along with the OOW and others, took up a position on the bridge and waited.

As the seconds ticked closer to H-hour, George could hear a low rumbling sound through the murky darkness of the early morning. At the same time, his Asdic operators reported increasing hydrophonic effects – the sound made by propellers. It was the reverberation of the approaching invasion fleet. Gradually the sound grew louder. In the pre-dawn light, dozens of shadowy shapes crystallized into lethal warships, their numbers filling the horizon. The invading fleet was massive, menacing, yet exciting. Amazingly, the previous day, they had sailed from Naples all the way to Anzio without being sighted by the enemy.

Then the relative silence was broken as the 6-inch guns of the cruisers opened up, saturating the beaches and targets further inland. The noise was tremendous, the spectacle electrifying. Shells whistled over George's head. Thousands of shells poured onto the landing area. Then, suddenly, the *Ultor* was surrounded by hundreds of vessels and landing craft making their way to the beach. George signalled details of the minefield found on the previous day.

A dense barrage of naval rockets preceded the troops. These were fired from two British LCTs (Landing Craft Tank) and made a deafening roar right up to the beach. These newly-developed rocket craft fired 5-inch rockets, each craft discharging 798 missiles. Hundreds of rockets were launched, starting about half a kilometre from the beach. The effect was brutal. Smoke and fire shattered the beach where they landed. The rockets kept firing steadily all the way up the beach, eventually 'sanitizing' a clear access lane. Then the first troops hit the beach. Landing craft dropped their ramps and disgorged hundreds of soldiers onto the now scarred earth.

George was resigned to the fact that he could do nothing more. He asked for some cocoa to be brought up to the bridge and he and several of the officers and men watched the battle unfold around them. It was a riveting scene – both epic and frightful. The invasion force caught the enemy by surprise. There was very little opposition and practically no retaliatory fire. George watched the first wave of men scramble up the beach and disappear into the trees.

Several hours later, a minesweeper manoeuvred through the maze of ships and stopped beside the *Ultor*. 'I'm your escort,' the Captain called to George. He recalled the dutiful Second Coxswain from the fo'c'sle and gave orders for the anchor to be weighed. His job was done – as was the *Ultor*'s. They followed the minesweeper through the fleet, sailing to the rear and moving towards the open sea. As she sailed past the flagship, the *Bulolo* (one of the Burns and Phillips

Line from Papua New Guinea), George and the crew were pleased to receive a flag signal from the Admiral: 'Well done'. It was followed by another message, this time communicated by signal lamp, '*Ultor* and *Uproar* take one day's leave at the Isle of Capri on the way back to La Maddalena.' Both messages were well received.

The submarines' role in the success of the invasion had indeed been critical. Their part in the operation was well planned and had gone like clockwork; the acknowledgements were therefore sincere.

Such was the complete surprise of the landings that the port of Anzio was captured virtually intact. By midday, the British were 2½ kilometres inland and the Americans had advanced to a depth of almost 5 kilometres. By the end of the day, 36,000 troops and 3,200 vehicles, tanks and trucks were safely ashore.

On their way back to Maddalena, both submarines, *Uproar* and *Ultor*, secured to the wharf at the Isle of Capri, which sits off the Gulf of Naples. This was a beautiful island. In peacetime, it was a well-known tourist spot, associated with fun, hedonism and Neapolitan love songs. Now it was an opportunity for the crew to have a real break. The shops were open and operating. There was good wine to be purchased and the restaurants supplied satisfying meals. There was also a chance to visit the ruins of the Imperial Roman villas and admire the views from the high panorama promenade.

George went for a cruise to visit the famous Blue Grotto cave, which he found interesting. He was also impressed with his visit to Gracie Fields' private villa near the Marina Piccola (small harbour). She had helped to make the island famous by singing 'The Isle of Capri'. The two days served to break the tension admirably and the men savoured the distraction as they knew that, within a few days, they would be back hunting for new prey.

CHAPTER FIFTEEN

Cape Camarat

By the beginning of February 1944, the Allies had pushed the Italian front further north, although the Anzio bridgehead had bogged down after initial impressive gains. A large Allied effort was now being aimed at cutting the German supply line.

The German Army in Italy was supplied almost entirely by the continental railway system which transported goods from Germany down through France and Austria. A small portion was conveyed by coastal shipping lines along the French Riviera and the Gulf of Genoa, mainly by Italian or French ships appropriated by the Germans. These included assorted landing craft, Siebel ferries and F-lighters. Protecting them, the German naval forces also had a U-boat base at Toulon as well as many anti-submarine vessels.

Allied surface naval forces concentrated their effort around Genoa, the Allied Air Forces attacked the railways and sea ports, while submarines from the Tenth Flotilla operated along the French Riviera. Four submarines left for patrols in this area during February. On the 5th, *Ultor* and *Uproar* put to sea with orders to scout around the Riviera – unbeknown to them, the patrol almost finished in tragedy. *Upstart* left on the 9th and *Untiring* on 14 February.

The *Ultor* cruised for several days, with the OOW searching intently for targets. It was *Ultor*'s tenth patrol and at this stage the submarine had acquired an impressive record: George and his crew had sunk at least eight vessels and taken part in a special operation at Anzio. The crew by now were very confident with each other and were indeed a well-oiled team.

When it came to attacking enemy shipping, George had developed his intuitive judgement and decision-making skills to a fine level. His experience and temperament allowed him to be calm under pressure, while his leadership and personality had by now earned the respect of his crew. His task had been made a little easier as only certain types of men were accepted to serve in submarines. Nonetheless, two of the qualities they had to possess were the ability to survive in cramped quarters for long periods of time, and tolerance.

George, the First Lieutenant and the Navigator and Torpedo Officer all lived in a small wardroom with four bunks, the fourth acting as a settee alongside the table. The four petty officers lived in a caboose the same size, and most of the crew lived out of hammocks slung above the ready-to-use torpedoes in their racks. Within seconds, they could convert their living quarters into action stations, ready for combat.

In the early hours of the morning of the 8th, having charged batteries and dived again, the crew were alerted by such an action call. While patrolling off Cape Camarat, at periscope depth, the OOW sighted a 4,000-ton merchant vessel, the *Venettio*, silhouetted beautifully in front of a brilliant rising moon. It would be a good target although it was accompanied by two destroyer escorts of 800 tons each, stationed one ahead and one astern of the *Venettio*. George ordered 'Diving Stations'.

The moonlight allowed for excellent visibility, the sea was calm and the weather fine. The three ships were moving in line ahead at 10 knots and presented fair game. George decided he would fire four torpedoes, aiming the first torpedo a half a length ahead of the *Venettio*, with the rest spread over two lengths. This way, he might hit one or more ships.

George realized it was going to be a long-range shot, but worth a try. At 3.24, and at a range of 6,000 yards, he started firing the torpedoes. They shot away from the *Ultor* at 9-, 14- and 15-second intervals, racing towards their target. The *Ultor* started to plane down to 200 feet and prepared for the inevitable counter-attack. Five minutes later, a tremendous explosion was heard. There was great elation in the *Ultor*, but George wasn't sure which ship he had hit; he would have to wait to find out as he knew the destroyers would act quickly.

Within a few minutes he was targeted himself when two depth charges were dropped and exploded nearby. The effect produced a concussive thump, rattling the boat, but causing no real damage. There might be more. George had already ordered 'Silent routine'. All engines and pumps were stabilized on rubber mountings and, while the ship was running on the batteries, as now, no sound was transmitted outside the hull. George himself wore sandals and most of the crew wore plimsolls (light rubber-soled canvas sports shoes).

They maintained this status for an hour. As usual there was no outward sign of any great stress, just a mild feeling of veiled tension. The crew were professionals. Most sat silently deep in thought; some talked quietly. The long seconds became minutes. Eventually, when it became obvious no more depth charges were going to be dropped, George brought the boat up to periscope depth. He saw the *Venettio*, which he had obviously missed, and one escort as they were moving towards the horizon, but one of the destroyers was missing. George assumed that that was the cause of the explosion. He would report it as being a 'probable', although he felt certain he had sunk it. (It was later confirmed through intelligence that he had indeed sunk the vessel.) It had been an unusual attack for it was not often that such brilliant moonlight, coupled with a flat calm sea, combined to make the conditions just right for a submerged attack at night.

In the meantime, *Uproar*, patrolling about 15 kilometres to the south, off the Hyeres Islands, had also heard the explosion. Not long afterwards the CO, Lieutenant Larry Herrick, a New Zealander, sighted the *Venettio*. As it was dark, he also attempted to attack her while *Uproar* was on the surface, but he was seen and was immediately fired upon by the remaining escort. The *Uproar* was forced to dive and waited for the expected depth-charge counter-attack, but none came. After a while, she surfaced and gave chase but it was too late, and she wasn't able to make contact again. *Venettio* escaped – twice in one night.

For the next week *Ultor* and *Uproar* continued to patrol their designated areas, with neither having any luck. On the afternoon of

15 February, the two boats were involved in a serious incident, one which could have finished in tragedy. While off the Gulf of St Tropez, about 10 kilometres from Cape Camarat, alarm bells rang for action in the *Ultor*. George had sighted an 80-ton modern sailing schooner. It was well laden and making heavy weather of it. There was no doubt it would be full of military stores and equipment. There were no escorts, so George acted immediately. To get closer, he took the *Ultor* right up to the edge of the zone bordering *Uproar*'s designated patrol area. He wasn't too concerned about approaching the edge of the area because he knew *Uproar* had been programmed to return home at least eight hours previously.

However, while George was watching the sailing vessel through his periscope and closing in to attack, to his horror, his lens focused on another periscope a mere 700 metres from him. It could be a U-boat. Reacting instantly, George gave the necessary orders to turn *Ultor* stern-on. This would be the safest course while he had a doubt in his mind. At the same time, he discussed the situation with his First Lieutenant, Barry Rowe.

'You know,' said George, 'I don't think it's a U-boat. I reckon it's probably Larry Herrick in the *Uproar*. He might not have gone yet.'

Rowe agreed. It was a gut feeling for both of them, prompted by the fact that it had happened before. The first submarine lost in the war had been the *Oxley*, a former Australian submarine that had been returned to the Royal Navy when Australia ended its submarine arm during the Depression. On 19 September 1939, a fortnight after war was declared, two British boats, the *Oxley* and the *Triton*, were based out of Dundee. While on patrol, they somehow became seriously out of position and garbled communications from the *Oxley* led to the *Triton* ramming the *Oxley* and sinking her with the loss of fifty-nine sailors.

Sticking to his intuition, George did not want to make a hasty decision. As the Asdic was normally only effective to about 2,000 metres, and the other boat was a great deal closer than that, he chose to take a calculated risk that this was not an enemy vessel. He said, 'I'll make the challenge.'

Using Morse code transmitted through the Asdic machine, the operator sent the challenge, or password, for the day. It was indeed

Uproar – she had not yet gone back to base in accordance with her orders as Herrick had decided to remain in the area for a few more hours. He had, in fact, also sighted the schooner and was angling for the best shot. The situation was dangerous and he realized the implications. He returned the correct reply to *Ultor's* challenge, followed by 'Sorry, yes, it's *Uproar.*'

Both boats would have to report the sighting in their patrol reports. There was no doubt his friend Lieutenant Herrick would be 'spoken to', as it *could* have been a serious matter.

Uproar then moved out of the area and headed for base while George moved back to the task in hand: to stalk and sink the enemy schooner. The vessel was not large enough to warrant a torpedo so he would sink it by gunfire. He ordered 'Gun Action Stations' and invited the gunlayer to study the vessel through the periscope. The *Ultor* closed in on the ship to within a few hundred metres, then, at 3.15pm, surfaced a little astern of it.

George climbed the conning tower ladder, opened the hatch and directed proceedings from the bridge. The gun crew followed and loaded the gun. Another sailor carried a .303 rifle. The Gunnery Officer, Lieutenant Mangnall, ordered, 'Stand by to open fire.'

The crew of the schooner reacted to the imminent action and quickly prepared to abandon ship by putting life rafts into the sea. George had a strict code: if the crew simply climbed into a lifeboat or jumped into the sea, they would not be fired upon. However, if there was any form of resistance, the Gunnery Officer would direct the rifleman to aim warning shots at the offending party or parties.

On George's orders, the 3-inch gun exploded into life. In quick succession, to orders from the Gunnery Officer, the gunlayer fired forty-three rounds at the hapless vessel, twenty of which smashed into the ship. Wood shattered and splintered as rounds crashed into the hull, others hitting the upper works and mast. Smoke began curling from the hold. Within seconds, the main mast and sails crashed down into a tangled mess on the deck, ropes and canvas sprawled over the sides of the ship. The boat began to take water and rapidly began to list and sink. Confusion reigned. Men yelled, some jumped, some swam, others cursed.

By 3.25 it was all over; the vessel disappeared into a watery grave. It was one way to sink a ship. This method was a useful exercise for the gun crew, but it was not as quick or efficient as placing an explosive charge on board, which many submarines were able to do. Once again, George wasn't overly concerned for the crew of the enemy vessel. They would either be picked up by one of their own ships or they could easily make it to land – territory held by the Germans. Importantly, the cargo and supplies would not be going to Italy.

In the meantime, *Untiring* had had an unfruitful patrol, but *Upstart* had achieved some success by sinking a German auxiliary minelayer off Toulon. She also had a narrow escape after a duel with a German U-boat and an aircraft. All four boats arrived back at Maddalena safely.

The following month, George would receive a different challenge in the Aegean.

CHAPTER SIXTEEN

The Aegean

March started off on a high note for George as he received news that he had been granted a Bar to his Distinguished Service Cross, for outstanding courage and skill while in command of HM Submarine *Ultor*. The award had been published in the *London Gazette* of 8 February 1944 and was a great start to the month as he celebrated with his friends.

At the beginning of March, the German garrisons in the Aegean were struggling. Supply lines from all sources to Crete, the Dodecanese and the Greek Islands had been drastically severed.

At this stage, there were five British submarines based at Malta, which was now home to the First Flotilla, and there were four operational submarines in the Greek Flotilla in Beirut. Together, the bulk of the Malta and Beirut patrols were concentrating their efforts in the Aegean.

On 1 March, *Ultor* and *Untiring* sailed for Malta, where the *Ultor* was being transferred to increase the pressure in the Aegean. The *Untiring* was to receive a periodical docking, leaving three boats, the *Uproar*, *Upstart* and *Universal* holding the fort at Maddalena.

On 7 March, George and *Ultor* left Malta with orders to patrol the north-west coast of Crete. To get into the Aegean was always difficult. The Germans had laid extensive minefields against surface vessels around most large ports and along the borders of the Aegean. In essence, the main minefields extended from Piraeus, the harbour at Athens, to Monemvasia Peninsula in the Peloponnese and across to Crete. The minefields were extensive and lethal. The mines were set to operate between 10 and 15 feet below the surface and were attached by cables to heavy drums sitting on the ocean floor. Individually, each mine consisted of a central sphere with horns protruding out at all angles, looking rather like a sinister medieval mace. The horns were fitted with a chemical, or other explosive device, so that if one of them were struck, the mine would explode.

To enter the Aegean, George approached a less protected area with a deep channel, near Suda Bay in Crete. As he neared this section, he planed the *Ultor* down to about 300 feet. Steadily and carefully he set a course under the minefield. It was a slow, nerve-racking operation. To conserve the batteries, *Ultor* could only proceed at about 2 or 3 knots. On at least two occasions, there was high tension in the boat as the crew heard very distinctly the sound of a mine mooring-wire scraping along the hull of the submarine. Blood ran cold as they were only too aware of the implications should the wire become entangled in the hydroplanes, or worse if it triggered the mine. It was scary stuff. (Reassuringly, the submarine was fitted with deflecting wires to minimize this happening, but the reality was always there.)

The whole process of moving under the minefields and out into the Aegean took about fourteen hours. Once safely through, the relief was palpable. George then began to reconnoitre around Andikithira (Antikythera) Island on the western edge of Crete.

It wasn't too long before he found that the area presented him with adequate targets, although the first ones were aggressive. Off Potamo, on 11 March, the *Ultor* was detected first by an R-boat – a small minesweeper often used for escort duty – and then by another small anti-submarine vessel, both of which rushed out of the harbour towards *Ultor*. George immediately went deep. The German vessels attacked instantly, dropping depth charges over the *Ultor*. The first few were dangerously close, shaking the submarine but not incurring any damage. In all, the enemy ships dropped fourteen depth charges on George and his crew – a rude welcome to the Aegean. George wrote in his patrol report: 'Received fourteen nicely placed depth charges . . . we were lucky.'

After the drubbing, George moved the *Ultor* from the area and proceeded to search further north. By 13 March, they were patrolling around the Peloponnese. This was the pattern of most patrols – an adrenalin rush, followed by long periods of comparative peace, then another adrenalin rush as an attack became imminent.

Around mid-afternoon on the 13th, the *Ultor* was engulfed by a wild rain squall, making conditions and visibility very difficult. They were off the east coast, off the village of Monemvasia, and George took her in for a closer inspection. Then, approaching from the Cape Kremidi direction, George sighted two F-lighters of 320 tons each. (F-lighters were used as coastal transports but were also efficient armed escort vessels, manned, of course, by Germans.)

George decided on a snap attack. He estimated the vessels were moving at 7 knots. He could gain some idea of this by listening to their propeller count and from other information passed on by the navigator, as well as timing the ships as they moved past the graticules of the periscope. (Graticules are small, vertical and horizontal, hair-like marks on the periscope lens.) He was 800 yards from his target. Visibility was poor, but at 3.29pm, he fired two torpedoes. They were individually aimed, but to his disgust, they both missed. Some minutes later the torpedoes were heard to explode on the beach 1,800 yards away. He realized the adverse conditions might have caused him to underestimate the speed of the F-lighters.

He didn't have to wait long for another opportunity. An hour later, while in the same area, he sighted another F-lighter. This one was stationary and sitting off Cape Paleo, making it a perfect target. By now the sea had calmed and the rain had stopped. The sky was overcast and the conditions presented him with clear visibility.

George advanced closer, bringing the *Ultor* in to a range of 850 yards. One torpedo would do it. He aimed directly amidships and at 4.51 fired the torpedo. It ran true and a few minutes later, a deafening explosion echoed back to the men in the *Ultor*. The crew's cheers were lost amid the blast as the vessel caught fire, exploded and blew itself in half. Within seconds, water raced in to the shattered aft section and it quickly sank, sliding to its final resting place in 25 fathoms of water. The forward section remained, splashing awash on the surface. Men were clinging to the wrecked craft, trying desperately to crawl through the carnage onto rafts, or grasping at floating debris. It would not take long for it to sink also. After missing the first two F-lighters, it was a satisfying result for the crew of the *Ultor*.

George continued his patrol for a few more days but sighted nothing worthwhile. He then undertook the arduous job of manoeuvring back under the minefields, and returned to Malta on 20 March.

On his return, he was given distressing news. Churchill had agreed with Roosevelt and Stalin to carve up Poland. The revelation had been devastating to the crew of the two Polish vessels, *Dzik* and *Sokol*. Both boats were based in Malta and were due to sail back to the United Kingdom for refits that month. Five years of fighting with unflinching bravery on the side of the Allies – who had gone to war in the first place following the German invasion of Poland – were for nought. They would have no home to go to now. As George knew most of the crew of the *Sokol* from his time in it as Liaison Officer, like most of the submariners in Malta, he was saddened by the decision.

There were plenty of targets remaining in the Aegean. During March, the other submarines in the Flotilla extracted a heavy toll on the Germans, sinking many vessels of all types. As there was still work to be done in this area, George and the *Ultor* did not have a long turnaround time. Within a few days, she had replenished her supplies and was reloaded with torpedoes. The *Ultor* left Malta in late March and soon found herself manoeuvring under the minefields again, heading back into the Aegean. On 3 April, she was sitting off the Island of Kithera (Kythera), at the southern tip of the Peloponnese.

Sailing near the entrance of the small port of Nikolo, George considered entering the harbour. He would have loved to have gone in, but he realized it would have been too small to negotiate. Regardless, he had a most successful day, eventually sinking four caiques by gunfire. The first two were 80-ton vessels loaded with German soldiers on their way to Crete. Using his now proven technique of surfacing close to a vessel and firing HEDA (High-Explosive Delayed Action) rounds, the caiques quickly broke up and sank into the harbour.

121

He approached a third caique of 30 tons and quickly sank her. Sailing closer to the port itself, he noticed a 60-ton caique resting on the building slip. It made an excellent target. After firing a few well-placed HEDA rounds, the vessel splintered and cracked, falling in on itself, the explosion completely wrecking it. In those few moments, the *Ultor* had sunk or demolished four caiques, leaving 250 tons of shipping destroyed in the harbour.

The next day, the *Ultor* moved around to the neighbouring island of Belo Pula where she encountered another caique of 40 tons. George ordered five HEDA rounds to be fired at the vessel, efficiently dispatching it in similar manner.

Two days later, on the 6th, the *Ultor* was off Port Kiparissi (Kyparissi) on Morea, (the early name for Peloponnese) where she came upon another caique of 50 tons. This one was a little more resistant and required fifteen HEDA rounds to finally sink her. Later in the day, George took the *Ultor* back to Belo Pula Island and found a 40-ton caique lying low in the water, clearly heavy with military stores.

George ordered 'Gun Action Stations', and surfaced to attack the vessel. The Gunnery Officer took charge and fired ten rounds. The early rounds steadily demolished the caique, but the last one revealed the true nature of her cargo. As it crashed into the vessel, the caique exploded violently, shooting splintered wood and metal high into the air. There was a deafening roar as the shell clearly hit the cargo of ammunition, creating blistering flashes of yellow and blue. Black smoke billowed into the air as fireworks screeched across the sky. Within a few minutes, the caique had completely disappeared.

But George and the *Ultor* were not finished with attacking caiques. The next morning, she was back off Monemvasia again. In light, choppy seas, while at periscope depth, George sighted a stationary, armed patrol caique of 200 tons, anchored in the harbour. The sky was cloudy but he had good visibility. George took the *Ultor* in to a range of 950 yards, aimed one torpedo amidships at the vessel and fired the torpedo.

The 'fish' raced just below the surface of the water and forty-three seconds later, smashed into the wooden vessel. Once again, the crash of shattering wood filtered back to the *Ultor*. It was a devastating explosion, instantly breaking the vessel in half. There was much confusion on the deck and in the water as sailors raced to escape the crippled ship; she was sinking fast. George recorded that the caique sank within six minutes. He also noted in his patrol report that there was a great deal of debris left in the water as shards of broken wood and equipment floated to the surface. The explosion had also brought out a number of spectators from the village and they were gathered on the beach to witness the event.

Some days later, George breached the minefields again and returned to Malta on 12 April. On this patrol he had sunk eight caiques totalling some 580 tons, with one torpedo and seventy-seven rounds of ammunition. This wholesale sinking of inter-island caiques should be seen in the context that the Germans, having occupied most of the Greek Islands, were almost completely dependent on caiques for supplies and the movement of their garrisons.

The attrition incurred by the *Ultor* and other submarines would have had a significant impact on the Germans. Well pleased with their record in the Aegean, the *Ultor* sailed for Maddalena.

This latest episode brought George's and the *Ultor*'s grand total of sunk and damaged enemy vessels to 25,030 tons – a great effort. This tonnage should be put into perspective. An archivist or historian might comment that sinking one decent-sized ship could destroy twice that tonnage, an observation that would have the potential to downgrade the significance of the *Ultor*'s achievements. What is important in the context of the war, at this stage, is to consider the number of ships that were sunk to create that tonnage. And, as has already been established, to impact to such effect on the enemy.

There was a lot more work to do yet in the Mediterranean.

CHAPTER SEVENTEEN

South Coast of France

May 1944 saw the 'Fighting Tenth' at Maddalena continuing to harass the enemy anti-submarine shipping off the south coast of France. George and the *Ultor* arrived back at Maddalena from Malta and service with the First Flotilla on 3 May, bringing the Tenth Flotilla up to its full strength again of five submarines.

After only two days in harbour, *Ultor* sailed for a patrol east of Hyeres Roads in southern France. This was about 30 kilometres east of Toulon, an area where some of the other submarines had already encountered a great deal of anti-submarine activity. On 11 May, George sighted a *Kriegstransporter* ship of 800 tons crawling slowly across the bay. She was obviously heavily stocked with equipment and supplies for the Italian front and was closely escorted by two E-boats.

Conditions were favourable for an attack. There was a fresh easterly wind blowing, the sea was moderate and the visibility good. At periscope depth, George approached the KT vessel to a range of 1,000 yards. From here, he fired two non-contact torpedoes, the first aimed just abaft the bow and the second just ahead of the stern.

Fifty-one seconds later, one of the torpedoes exploded directly underneath the hull. It had the desired effect. With a tremendous crash, the force 'lifted' the KT ship, breaking its back so that the vessel broke in half. It did not take long for her to sink. George expected a strong counter-attack from the two escorts as he had snatched his prize from right under their noses. The *Ultor* went deep immediately and waited silently. To George's surprise and relief they did not retaliate, and no depth charges were dropped.

George continued patrolling around the southern coast area for the next two days. On the early evening of the 15th, off Cape Lardier, the OOW spotted a deeply laden 80-ton motor vessel, a 'coaster' as it was known. (Some time later, the Admiralty Weekly Intelligence Report called the encounter 'a welcome novelty'.) George decided to attack the vessel with his gun.

The *Ultor* surfaced about 1,500 yards from the vessel. George ordered the gunlayer to open fire. Very quickly, the damage to the coaster became significant. The Captain must have realized he couldn't save his ship so he steered the vessel towards the coastline. As the coaster crunched onto the rocky shore, George could see the crew abandoning her. At this stage, the *Ultor's* gunners had fired nineteen rounds and George's intention was to demolish the vessel completely. However, suddenly, George heard the crash of other guns opening up – the *Ultor* was being fired upon. Enemy shore batteries had witnessed the event and had commenced firing at the *Ultor*. Shells flew overhead and some crashed into the sea not far from the *Ultor*, sending plumes of water high into the air.

George couldn't risk having the *Ultor* hit so he broke off the attack, pressed the diving klaxon and clattered down the ladder to the control room. Within seconds the well-drilled team had *Ultor* submerged and out of harm's way.

The Maddalena submarines did well in May. Together, they sank one *Kriegstransporter* ship, two of the three German ships that were known to be trading with Spain and two anti-submarine vessels.

The following month, June, would be the most momentous for the progress of the war, and George's next two patrols would be the most eventful of his submarine career.

CHAPTER EIGHTEEN

Cassis

As May 1944 drew to a close, the enemy was feeling strongly the pressure on their Italian front. To supply their troops, they were still using the sea route from Marseilles and Toulon, across to Leghorn in northern Italy. So the submarines still had plenty of targets.

George and *Ultor* left for their fourteenth patrol before the end of May. His main orders were to search around the Toulon area. He was also asked to assess the swept channel into Toulon.

The Allied landings in Normandy were imminent and it was proposed that a diversionary landing would be carried out somewhere in this area in the south of France – Operation ANVIL. The hope was to deceive the Germans that the Allies were going to land there in strength and to convince the enemy to concentrate their troops in this area, distracting their attention from the main game in northern France. This was one of the lessons the Allied Command had learned from the tragic Dieppe Raid in 1942.

On 29 May, the *Ultor* was lying off Toulon. For three days, George had been observing two 150-ton minesweepers coming in and out of Toulon. He noticed that they would sweep the channels, then return to their dock a little south of Cassis. He was impressed by their typical German thoroughness: they would follow exactly the same routine every day – same time, same methodical procedures. This enabled George to plot all the details of the Toulon approaches, including the channels regularly swept for mines.

He would watch as they proceeded in line abreast, towing a specially serrated wire between them. The procedure, when dealing with moored mines, was to snag and cut a mine's anchor wire, causing the mine, which was buoyant, to float to the surface. From here it would be sunk by rifle fire from one of the minesweepers.

George had planned to continue monitoring these two vessels on the 30th; however, during the early hours of that morning, he was distracted by the sudden presence of potential multiple targets. The *Ultor* was at periscope depth off Cape Camarat when George noticed five light craft coming into his vision, escorted by three R-boats. Turning the periscope lens onto high power, he realized the convoy consisted of a powerful 1,000-ton armed salvage tug towing a 400-ton lighter; these were accompanied by three smaller F-lighters. It was an interesting group.

Conditions were suitable for an attack. There was a slight easterly wind and the sea generated a moderate swell; visibility was good. George took the *Ultor* to a position on the landward side, about 1,500 yards from the tug. The convoy now presented a continuous target. He ordered four torpedoes to be brought to the ready. He would spread the four torpedoes over three of the vessels: the tug, one of the F-lighters and the lighter under tow.

At 6.57am, George started firing the torpedoes, each individually aimed. Less than a minute later, he watched through the periscope as one of the torpedoes smashed into the tug. As he was a fair distance away, he didn't go deep immediately, preferring to watch the scene. It was a direct hit, causing an explosion on board the tug. There was pandemonium around the stricken vessel as men and boats jostled to save lives. It didn't take long for the tug to sink. George then took the *Ultor* deep, anticipating some form of retaliation from the escorts.

Within a few minutes, the escort ships carried out a half-hearted depth-charge counter-attack, but they didn't make a serious attempt as they only dropped five depth charges in one pattern, none of which exploded close to the *Ultor*.

After about thirty minutes, George brought the *Ultor* to periscope depth to check on the situation. He noticed one of the R-boats was moving across to the 400-ton lighter which had previously been towed by the tug and decided to watch it for a while. At the same time, he ordered another torpedo to be loaded and brought to the ready.

Within a few minutes, the R-boat moved alongside the lighter, whereupon George moved in closer to the two enemy ships and waited about 800 yards away. His heart beat a little faster as he stared through the periscope at the unusual target. He set the torpedo with a CCR non-contact pistol (this would allow the torpedo to explode without contact) and aimed amidships at the stationary vessels, now lying side by side.

At 8.36am, George fired the torpedo. He remained watching and, less than thirty seconds later, the torpedo exploded under both ships. There was a tremendous explosion as the two vessels were momentarily lifted out of the water. Smoke, flames and debris burst away from the climactic scene. This was a rare event – two with one shot! George relayed the news to his crew, which resulted in great excitement. He asked the Navigating Officer to take a photograph through the periscope for the record.

Both ships sank very quickly leaving a large number of buoys and much wreckage floating on the surface. George had no doubt the vessel had been taking anti-torpedo nets to a nearby harbour. For some reason, the two remaining R-boats didn't mount a counter-attack.

The *Ultor* continued her patrol. Their Jolly Roger would be even more impressive, but the patrol and the action weren't over yet.

The next day, the 31st, the *Ultor* returned to continue observing the two minesweepers off Toulon. They were now south of Cassis and, late in the day, his observations complete, George decided he would sink one. He waited until the evening when the minesweepers were in line abreast and had stopped sweeping. Behind them, on Verte Island, was a coastal battery of guns which he would have to watch as they could be a threat to his boat. The *Ultor* was in shallow waters, but George decided it was worth the risk to order a gun attack and passed the command, 'Gun action stations'.

As the sun was setting, George surfaced the *Ultor* within 1,000 yards of the nearest minesweeper. *Ultor* was well covered by darkness while the minesweepers were silhouetted against the setting sun, presenting a clear target. George ordered the Gunnery Officer to stand by. At 10.20pm, the gun began firing. The crash of the gunfire and the sound of the exploding HEDA rounds shattered the stillness of the night.

Within a few minutes, the gunlayer had fired twenty-five rounds, fourteen of which hit the nearest minesweeper, creating a great deal of damage. The vessel spontaneously caught fire and lit up the sky like a bonfire. It burned fiercely, the yellow flames and black smoke initially preventing the other minesweeper lurking behind it from firing at the *Ultor*. Within a few minutes, the stricken minesweeper blew up in a spectacular display and sank quickly. The attack was going well.

George prepared to order the gun to fire at the second minesweeper, but before he could do so, his signalman turned to him and pointed to a commotion on the shore behind the ships – on the corniche. The corniche was a beautiful strip of narrow road that ran right along the water's edge. Cars had stopped, the occupants had left their vehicles and were milling around, trying to observe the dramatic scene being played out in front of them.

The signalman asked George, 'How about I spray them with the Vickers, Sir?' (a machine gun mounted on the conning tower).

There was no indication to George that the crowd were military, so he replied, 'Oh, come on. You can't do that. They're all civilians and some may be kids!'

But it was too late anyway. By now, the shore batteries had come to life and began firing at the *Ultor*, the first few shells dangerously close, crashing into the water nearby. At the same time, the remaining minesweeper had got under way and started chasing the *Ultor*, firing as it went.

It was definitely time to get out of there. George urgently ordered everybody down from the gun and off the bridge, back down into the submarine. He remained alone on the bridge and called a message down the voice pipe to Charlie Pels, the Navigating Officer, 'Remain closed up at Diving Stations.' He quickly followed this directive with the orders, 'Steer 180 degrees back out to sea. Watch the echo sounder and as soon as the depth gets to one hundred feet, we'll dive.'

For the moment, they were keeping their distance. They could actually move faster on the surface, about the same speed as the minesweeper, which gave them a good start.

George kept in close contact with the Navigating Officer below. The depth sounder was 'pinging', relaying the depth of water back to the latter. The equipment was extremely sensitive, emitting just enough energy to reflect from the sea bottom.

Then, suddenly, George's luck ran out. A small-calibre shell from the minesweeper crashed onto the *Ultor*, smashing into the front of the bridge. It had hit a section constructed of brass, not far from where George was standing and the impact shook him momentarily. (This section was specially built from non-ferrous metal. In the event of the regular gyro compass or electrics breaking down, a magnetic compass, known as 'Faithful Freddie', could be placed near this brass section, allowing the compass to work properly.)

The shell sent shrapnel splinters flying in all directions. One small brass piece sliced into George's right thigh, although he could see that the wound was probably not serious as it seemed to be little more than a flesh wound along his inner thigh. Mercifully, and to his relief, it had missed the 'crown jewels'. But it was close and it was bleeding.

At this point Pels, the Navigating Officer, called up the voice pipe to report a depth of fifteen fathoms (90 feet, or 27.6 metres) – which was near enough for the order to dive to be given.

George steadied himself and pressed the diving klaxon before briskly shutting the hatch after him and scrambling down the conning tower into the control room. The Coxswain brought a first aid kit and a bandage was applied to his thigh. For the time being, the bleeding was under control.

The *Ultor* made good her escape. Luckily, they were not followed by any depth-charge attack.

The next day, George had a chance to assess his injury which luckily was little more than a flesh wound. The bleeding had stopped and, even though the wound was uncomfortable, he was able to remain on his feet.

The patrol wasn't over yet as they had orders to move south, past the Gulf of Lyon, to the Franco-Spanish border. It took a day to travel there and on the early morning of 2 June, the *Ultor* was situated 10 kilometres from the border, lying at periscope depth off Port Vendres.

Coming out of the harbour, George sighted a perfect target: the *Alice Robert*, a 5,000-ton, heavily-armed merchant ship, which the Germans were using as a minelayer. She was escorted by a destroyer of the Le Terrible class. Both vessels were formidable opponents. By now, George had his three remaining torpedoes loaded ready for action.

George took the *Ultor* inshore to a range of 2,000 yards. At 8.34am, he fired the three torpedoes and then went deep. Eighty seconds later, one torpedo was heard to hit the target. It was a significant explosion and George decided that perhaps some of the mines the *Alice Robert* was carrying might have blown up. The crew of the *Ultor* didn't have long to wait for a counter-attack – exactly fifteen minutes later, depth charges began exploding in set patterns around them. Fifteen were dropped in total, but no damage was done.

At 9.10am, George brought *Ultor* up to periscope depth and searched for evidence of the outcome of his attack. There was no sign of the *Alice Robert* which had most likely gone to the bottom. The destroyer was searching for the *Ultor* but had moved away in another direction. In the area where the enemy vessel had been, George could see boats and other enemy vessels picking up men from the ocean. It was a good result.

He had no more torpedoes so it was time to go home.

On his arrival back at Maddalena, George was able to have his injury treated. The piece of shrapnel in his thigh was extracted and the wound was tended and stitched. The prognosis was good.

He and the crew of the *Ultor* were also greeted with some heartening news of the progress of the war. In Italy, the Allied armies had advanced and joined up at the Anzio bridgehead. On 4 June, they captured Rome. Even more importantly, on 6 June, the Allies began their invasion of Europe with the Normandy landings. The tide was definitely turning.

To add to the good news, George heard that he had been awarded a second Mention in Dispatches (MiD). This had been gazetted on 9 May 1944 and was for the reconnaissance and beach-marking while in command of the *Ultor* at Anzio, and subsequently acting as a beacon for the assault force as they approached the beaches.

By 16 June, George was fully fit and took the *Ultor* on her fifteenth patrol, one that would prove to be the most eventful, arduous and successful of all.

CHAPTER NINETEEN

Nice

On 15 June 1944, just before he left for his fifteenth patrol, George was distressed to find he was to be denied the services of his trusted First Lieutenant, Barry Rowe. On this occasion, George was in the staff office discussing recent intelligence concerning Nice, the area they would be patrolling.

During the briefing, an old friend of George's, Lieutenant Paddy Gowan, came into the office. They had been friends since they were 14, back in HMS *Conway* days when they were officer cadets. Gowan was now Commanding Officer of the spare crew at the base, and was desperate to get to sea. He spoke to George.

'Sorry to have to tell you this but Barry Rowe has gone sick and is being operated on tomorrow. But not to worry. I'll come as your First Lieutenant instead.'

That was a real bonus for George. To have Gowan on board would be very good, but he would miss Rowe. He went immediately to visit Rowe after the briefing and commiserated with him.

The *Ultor* sailed the next day and soon established a patrol off the Golfe de la Napoule (Cannes). George found there was considerable anti-submarine activity in the region.

On the 19th, while off Nice, he sighted a tug towing an R-boat. It was a small target, so George closed the range to increase his chances of success – unfortunately the *Ultor* went in too close, and the R-boat Captain noticed the *Ultor's* periscope and fired on it. George immediately took *Ultor* down to 200 feet and ordered 'Silent routine'.

For two hours, the *Ultor* was hunted by the escort. It was a deadly cat-and-mouse game, but the R-boat only dropped one depth charge. Eventually, with great relief, George was able to break free and quietly moved *Ultor* out of the area.

Very early the next morning, 20 June, while deep, they became aware that two destroyers and a UJ-boat (a specialized anti-submarine hunter) had passed directly overhead. They therefore reverted to 'silent routine' again and were not detected.

Three hours later, while at periscope depth, the OOW identified a potential target, an F-lighter of 320 tons. It was escorted by an R-boat and suddenly appeared as the two vessels sailed around from behind a point of land. The F-lighter was bristling with anti-aircraft guns. The weather was calm and fine, allowing good visibility. George decided on a snap attack. He took *Ultor* in to a range of 1,000 yards and ordered two torpedoes to be made ready. He aimed one just inside the bow, and the second at the stern.

The attack lasted only twelve minutes. At 7.51am George fired the first of the two torpedoes. Less than a minute later one torpedo was definitely heard to hit the lighter, although it seemed that the second torpedo must have missed. Regardless, the result was devastating to the enemy vessel. It exploded on impact, simply being 'blown to bits', smoke, flame and debris being hurled into the sky. George watched the irresistible scene for several minutes at periscope depth. Six minutes after the attack all that was remaining afloat was a portion of the bow.

He then watched the R-boat for some time as it moved among the floating wreckage picking up survivors. He was considering putting a shot into it as well when a UJ-boat appeared from behind the nearby island of St Marguerite. It was time to go. The *Ultor* went deep and headed towards the open sea to reload her torpedoes.

For the next week, patience was needed as real action was fairly quiet. There was still some anti-submarine activity, but nothing worthwhile or close enough to attack. But that was about to change.

In the very early hours of the morning of 27 June, the *Ultor* had surfaced in the dark and was recharging her batteries. George had made the decision, as this was their last day on patrol, that they would spend it off Nice.

At 4.15am, the Asdic operator reported picking up the beat of propellers – something was approaching from the east. George immediately ordered 'Diving stations' and down they went to periscope depth so that he could study the ships against a background of the emerging dawn light. Through the periscope, George detected a shape, but it was too dark to identify any particular target. By 4.45am, however, he knew he was dealing with a convoy. Five minutes later, silhouetted against the increasing light, he was able to identify a large 3,000-ton merchant vessel escorted by three destroyers and a corvette. He was in business.

The target was an old 'three-island' merchant ship with a straight stem. Such ships were designed to have a large cargo-carrying capacity. It was painted black with white upper bodywork and was moving quite slowly – about 6 knots – so slowly that the escorts were weaving. As they were only about 5 kilometres south of Villefranche, their most likely intended port, they were 'marking time' until it became light.

George decided to move as close inshore as he could to achieve his best shot, although this would be difficult because of the weaving escorts. He was going to have to get inside them. The *Ultor* went deep and carefully crossed under and ahead of the starboard side of one of the destroyers, managing to avoid detection. Now George was inside the screen. This was dangerous territory, so patience and resolve were vital.

He then took *Ultor* in to 1,000 yards range. It was still quite dark, although the target was clearly silhouetted against the first rays of the rising sun. The sea was calm; he was ready to attack. To cover possible errors in calculating the enemy's course and speed, George spread four torpedoes over two lengths. At 5.04am he fired his salvo and dived deep. Forty seconds later, two of them were heard to smash into the vessel.

There was no reaction for a full minute. The crew looked curiously at each other, but all of a sudden there was a tremendous crash and the ship blew up with one of the loudest explosions George had heard. He was sure the ship must have contained munitions. For several minutes, as the stricken ship began to break up, loud rumblings, creakings and crashes echoed back from the wreck. Then there was nothing – just silence. George was sure she had sunk.

Realizing vengeance would be swift, George began to move the *Ultor* south to escape the impending battering, but he wasn't fast enough. Within ten minutes of unleashing the torpedoes, the first depth charges exploded near them, followed very quickly by others. The hunters were persistent as still more explosions rocked the submarine.

In the meantime, the Asdic operator had picked up some other hydrophone effects and Asdic impulses. George concluded that the four escorts might have been reinforced by extra anti-submarine vessels. The depth charges kept on coming, both singly and in patterns.

George was aware that he must reload his last two torpedoes as soon as possible, but not while being hunted. Chains were needed to move a ton-and-a-half torpedo, which was very noisy. The *Ultor* stayed deep and on 'silent routine'.

In all, forty depth charges were dropped, the most intensive pounding George had so far experienced. The enemy knew the submarine should be close and were keen to destroy it but eventually, the pummelling eased; George was relieved that no real damage had occurred.

After a while, George discussed with Gowan the merits of sending the crew to breakfast or whether to reload the torpedoes into the tubes. It was not possible to do both because the sailors lived and ate where they would need to manoeuvre the torpedoes. As they were still being hunted, they decided they should not start reloading and have breakfast instead.

Later, at 6.10am, George decided to assess the situation on the surface. He brought the *Ultor* up to periscope depth and, to his surprise, spotted five aircraft circling overhead. They were enemy aircraft and were obviously escorts, but he couldn't immediately identify what they were protecting.

In the distance, he could see the four enemy escorts he had earlier been trying to avoid, the three destroyers and a corvette, temporarily out of the way. He now had time to reload so he ordered the fore end of the submarine to be stripped. This was the area where the torpedoes were stored and where the crew had just finished breakfast. All lockers and tables were moved in readiness to start reloading the torpedoes, a process that could take fifteen to thirty minutes, depending on the number of torpedoes to be loaded.

Just then, at 6.55am, before the crew could commence reloading, to his astonishment he sighted a tanker to the south-west, just off Cape Antibes. He could also see the masts and upper works of several other vessels – another convoy was coming. He reckoned they were probably heading for Nice and quickly called for a crash reload of the remaining two torpedoes.

By 7.25am, one torpedo had been reloaded. By now it was broad daylight and perfect conditions for an attack. This gave George a chance to scrutinize the tanker. It was large, and very slow, proceeding at only about 4 knots. George was puzzled by this until he realized that she was being towed by two tugs. He also noted she had five escorts – a destroyer, a corvette, a large UJ-boat and two R-boats. The five aircraft circling overhead were also acting as escorts. This would be a challenging attack.

George became more concerned, however, when he saw that the four escorts of his previous victim were also heading south-west to join the tanker escorts. This would bring the screen to nine ship escorts and five aircraft, a formidable force. With only two torpedoes left, George would have to penetrate the lot and get in close.

In George's favour was the slow speed of the tanker. The escorting vessels were moving at a much higher speed and were also weaving in such an exaggerated fashion, sometimes turning a complete circle, that they were churning up the water dramatically, enough to confuse and 'mask' their own Asdics.

Against this, however, his first difficulty was that he simply *had* to stay at periscope depth so that he could actually see – a teeth-gritting problem in itself and very dangerous. An alert OOW on any of the enemy ships, or any sailor for that matter, might well spot his periscope at any moment. On the other hand, to offset this disadvantage, the white water kicked up by the escorts would help to cover his periscope.

Going deep to avoid being rammed was not an option, as he normally would with any approaching escort. If he went deep, his Asdic would not give him a precise picture of the position of each escort, and he would be unclear as to where or when to return safely to periscope depth. It would be sheer luck to come up without being rammed by one of the escorts as their movements were so erratic.

After much deliberation, George slowly took the *Ultor* forward, between the two leading escorts and the starboard bow destroyer. The whole time he was intently watching all the other nearby escorts, as well as keeping a discreet look at the skies for the circling aircraft. His hands gripped the controls tightly while he swivelled the periscope to all angles. For each search, he could only risk raising and looking through the periscope for two or three seconds to avoid being seen.

Suddenly, he was inside the screen. The situation in the control room was tense. George had passed on a verbal commentary of the proceedings to the crew and they were all on the highest alert level.

'Everybody has to be absolutely on their toes. We've just penetrated a very strong screen,' he warned them.

For the first time, George had a clear view of the tanker. It was large, about 5,000 tons, painted grey and almost half-loaded with cargo. It was now 8.15am and the second torpedo had been loaded. He ordered the torpedoes set to 16 feet, aimed to go off at about keel depth, or under it if she was drawing less water than he estimated.

He was under pressure from one of the escorts. The destroyer on his starboard quarter gave him several frights as it surged up close, nearly on the beam of the *Ultor*.

'Don't look down now,' he muttered to the OOW and lookouts on the enemy destroyer. He was also well aware that he could not predict the next move of any of the escorts. His luck was holding, but for how long? The sooner he fired the better.

He brought the *Ultor* in to a range of 1,500 yards. Instead of waiting to position himself at right angles on the beam for the best shot, he needed to get his torpedoes away as soon as possible. He aimed for the break of the forecastle and the poop on a 75-degree track. At 8.31am, he fired both torpedoes.

Sixty-nine seconds later, both torpedoes smashed into the tanker. They had done it.

George immediately decided to go deep. Over the next thirty seconds, the *Ultor* planed down to 300 feet, approaching its maximum safe depth. The crew shut off everything in readiness for the imminent depth-charge assault (this included shutting off all inlets and outlets, including the toilet), and went into 'silent routine'. Now they would play out the waiting game as they were well aware that the hunt for them would be on in earnest. They were, after all, still surrounded by nine angry escort vessels, with aircraft above them.

It didn't take long for the first of the depth charges to arrive. Within a few minutes, explosions were crashing all around them, shaking the submarine and its occupants. The water bubbled and frothed on the surface as the escorts furiously worked in patterns, hurtling the charges all around the immediate area. Some were dangerously close.

One concussive burst shattered the external port and starboard navigational lights. Another twisted the dipoles on the radar mast and pushed them out of true. Inside the submarine, men gripped whatever they could to steady themselves. A further nearby blast caused a number of electric lights to flash out, some gauges shattered and, unfortunately, the stern glands again started to leak. Crockery fell and smashed.

The hammering continued relentlessly for over an hour as the *Ultor* endured about 100 depth charges tossed at her. This was traumatic stuff, but that was what the crew were trained for. Every man concentrated on his job. All the while, using only one propeller, quiet as a mouse, the *Ultor* was steadily and silently creeping away from the scene, maintaining about 3 knots. George had learnt a long time ago that there was no merit in moving away from the action at high speed – the enemy's Asdics would soon pick him up.

Eventually, the bombardment ceased and the hunting seemed to have quietened down. Comparatively little actual damage had been done to the *Ultor*, the most serious being the stern glands. The pressure at 300 feet made the leak worse, so it was imperative that

George returned the submarine to periscope depth. When he did, the leak was reduced considerably. He considered they were extremely lucky.

To his amazement, he found the escorts had all given up and he could see that the tanker was stopped and dead in the water. It had a broken back and the bow and stern were cocked up out of the water, sitting like a giant 'V'. When he passed this information on to the crew, the tension evaporated and there was a hearty round of cheers. It had been one of the most tense, exacting and rewarding victories they had experienced.

George had some periscope photos taken and invited several of the crew to witness the results of their handiwork. This was a great morale booster, as about eight sailors grinned with satisfaction at the sight of the stricken enemy vessel – one step closer to finishing the war. He was particularly pleased to invite Petty Officer Trewhela to the periscope, the Torpedo Gunner's Mate. He, along with his team, had lovingly cared for each of the sixty-six torpedoes that they had fired so far. Trewhela, a Cornishman, always blew a kiss to each one before it went on its way, so he was thrilled to view the damaged ship and spent several seconds at the lens.

As members of the crew watched, some shore gun batteries opened up on the stricken ship. The enemy had obviously decided that the now deserted remaining part of the tanker would allow them some good practice. By 10.00am, what remained of their victim had been sunk, but the escorts had not given up their hunt and were still actively searching for the *Ultor*. George again went deep and, after another two hours' nail-biting tension, the *Ultor* finally shook them off at noon.

Having expended all his torpedoes, George signalled his situation to base and set course for 'home'. By next morning, they arrived back at Maddalena. George was delighted to find Barry Rowe waiting at the jetty to meet them. He was also pleased to note in his report, with great satisfaction, that Paddy Gowan had not forgotten any of his First Lieutenant's expertise, and had done a perfectly splendid job. It really had been good to be together again after all those years as cadets.

He was also impressed to find that the intelligence, mainly from the French Resistance, was so effective that they were able to tell George the names of the ships he had just sunk. The first one was the German-requisitioned former French cargo ship, *Cap Blanc*, and the tanker was the *Pallas*.

Some time later, the Captain of the Tenth Submarine Flotilla, Captain P.Q. Roberts, when officially forwarding the patrol report to the Commander-in-Chief, Mediterranean, wrote in glowing terms on the attack:

The attack on the 3,000 ton merchant ship was brilliantly carried out, but I have no hesitation in saying that, in my considerable experience of submarining, the attack on the tanker only three hours later is the most superlative exhibition I have ever heard. That Lieutenant Hunt should achieve an unseen, undetected position at 1,500 yards inside such a massive and violently zig-zagging screen suggests consummate technical skill, but shows, moreover, determination and courage of the highest order … Lieutenant Hunt very seriously described the screen and their manoeuvres to me on his return as 'very off-putting', a rather attractive understatement … A performance that will be difficult for his own or any other submarine to rival.

CHAPTER TWENTY

Cape Lardier

June 1944 had been a remarkable month for the Tenth Flotilla. Between them, the four active submarines, *Ultor*, *Universal*, *Untiring* and *Upstart* made eleven attacks, ten of which were successful. Displaying splendid marksmanship during these attacks, they fired thirty-two torpedoes, sixteen of which hit their target. Their tally credited them with sinking four large merchant vessels, two lighters, a salvage vessel, a minelayer and five smaller armed vessels.

Overall, the Mediterranean war effort was going well. By the end of June, the Allied armies in Italy had reached the coast abreast of Elba and the French had now occupied the island. The enemy's coastline was contracting fast. Meanwhile Operation ANVIL, the invasion of southern France, had been postponed. The original plan was for it to proceed simultaneously with Operation OVERLORD, the Normandy landings on 6 June, but there were not enough landing craft left in the Mediterranean. It had now been rescheduled to go ahead for August.

By July, substantial numbers of American troops had been transferred from Italy for Operation ANVIL. It was now more important than ever to prevent supplies reaching the German Army. There was a massive American air attack on 5 July on German U-boats based in Toulon; one U-boat was sunk and two others were damaged.

However, there was always sobering news to remind submariners of the deadly risks involved. When George returned from his fifteenth patrol on 29 June, he was greeted with the information that the *Sickle*, one of the First Flotilla's S-class submarines from Malta, was missing with its full complement of officers and men. It was thought the boat had probably struck a mine. *Sickle* was the forty-fifth British submarine to be sunk in the Mediterranean. Submariners accounted for one of every three naval personnel killed in this war – a high price for success.

On 18 July, George in the *Ultor* sailed for their sixteenth patrol in the Mediterranean. It was to be their last. George had orders to search from Hyeres Island to Cape Roux, an area he now knew well. He was also ordered to carry out further reconnaissance for Operation ANVIL, the impending landings in the south of France.

On the evening of the 21st, while patrolling off Cape Lardier at periscope depth, he sighted a 500-ton coaster, *UJ2211*. It had one escort, a German-requisitioned French *chasseur*. As the weather was calm and the sea lazy, George decided it should be his next target. He approached to a range of 800 yards and ordered two non-contact torpedoes to be prepared for firing. Just before 8.50pm, with a blast of compressed air behind them, the torpedoes raced towards their target.

Thirty-four seconds later, one torpedo smashed into the ship. It was a direct hit, causing the vessel to fill quickly with water. George was mindful of the escort, but she made no attempt to counter-attack. Instead, the *chasseur* stayed at the scene and picked up survivors as the coaster sank.

George then took *Ultor* around to some of the beaches east of Toulon and Nice. Here, for the next three days, his mine detection unit investigated the seas off the Gulf of Fréjus and St Tropez. The Asdic operators 'pinged' continuously, searching for mines. They found an extensive minefield, and plotted and recorded the information.

At this stage, the submarine suffered technical faults in one of the main motor armatures and it was futile trying to continue. On 26 July, George took the *Ultor* back to base.

The landings in the south of France were now definitely set to take place in mid-August and preparations were being made all over the western Mediterranean. *Ultor* and *Ultimatum* had brought back valuable information concerning the enemy's defensive minefields, but the actual landing plans required no direct help from submarines.

The Tenth Flotilla's operations in the Mediterranean were being scaled down. Both *Ultor* and *Ultimatum* had already made their last patrols and were due for refit in the United Kingdom. Only two patrols were made from Maddalena in August, by *Curie* and *Universal*, and they were completed by 11 August, leaving the area clear for the invasion of the south of France.

While George and the *Ultor* were preparing to leave for the United Kingdom, the invasion took place on 15 August. Reports came back that the landings were entirely successful. Meanwhile, the submarines of the Tenth Flotilla lay quietly in their base at Maddalena.

Before *Ultor* returned home, the Commander-in-Chief, Mediterranean, J.H.D. Cunningham noted, 'Considering the paucity of targets off the south coast of France this year, the successes achieved by *Ultor* have been most outstanding and are due to the consistently conspicuous daring of her Commanding Officer.'

George was particularly pleased to be told of another report from the Commander-in-Chief, Mediterranean, to the Admiralty:

> For the information of their Lordships. Great credit to the Commanding Officer of HM Submarine *Ultor*, Lieutenant G.E. Hunt, DSC*, RN, for this most satisfactory patrol during which one 'F' lighter, one 3,000 ton motor vessel and one tanker were sunk. HM Submarine *Ultor*'s actions on the morning of 27th June rank with some of the most outstanding of the war.

This was reinforced by a Top Secret signal from the Admiralty, addressed to the Commander-in-Chief, Mediterranean:

> Please convey the congratulations of the Board of Admiralty to the Captain and Ship's Company of H.M. Submarine *Ultor* on the outstanding success of her recent patrols.

Not long after these messages were received and after some heartfelt goodbyes, *Ultor* and *Ultimatum* left for the UK, soon to be followed by *Universal*. The remaining submarines (there were now three others) were transferred to different bases in early September, the base at Maddalena was closed down and the famous Tenth Flotilla was finally disbanded on 21 September 1944.

The *Ultor*'s achievements in the Mediterranean had been remarkable. It had attained the highest number of ships sunk by any British submarine during the war. Lieutenant Commander David Wanklyn VC, in *Upholder*, sank the most tonnage of any British commanding officer. (It is worth pointing out that Wanklyn sank his vessels in the early part of the war, including some large Italian liners, which quickly racked up an impressive tonnage. In the process, he did not leave too many for the following years.)

During her seventeen patrols, *Ultor* had sunk or destroyed over 50,000 tons of Axis shipping. Admiralty records of 5 September 1944 show twenty vessels sunk and two damaged by torpedo, and ten sunk by gunfire (including one destroyed on the stocks), giving a total of thirty vessels sunk and two damaged. In addition, *Ultor* took part in one bombardment, one beach-marking and one special operation.

To assist in achieving this record, *Ultor* carried out twenty-seven torpedo attacks, of which twenty-three were successful, a success rate of 85.2 per cent. She fired sixty-eight torpedoes, of which thirty-two were hits (plus two possibles), a success rate of 47 per cent, which was the highest rate of any British submarine. George himself, counting his time in submarines before *Ultor*, had carried out no less than thirty-two patrols.

In terms of ships sunk and destroyed, George was now recognized as one of the leading British submarine captains of the war. With this proud record behind them, George and his company sailed for Gibraltar. On the way, they called in at Algiers, where George had an interesting experience when he noticed lying in the pens in the corner of the dockyard a large number of destroyers. He boarded the depot ship and found the chief yeoman.

'Those are all Italian destroyers?' he asked. (They were now, of course, Allied co-belligerents.)

'Yes, Sir.'

'Have you got a list of their names?'

'Yes, Sir.'

George searched through the names and when he discovered that one of them was *Sagittario*, he arranged to be taken over to her. Once aboard, he found the Engineer Officer and asked him, 'Is there anybody on board from when the ship rammed a submarine in the Aegean in 1941?'

The officer replied, 'Yes, Sir, I was. We sank the submarine.'

George replied, with a wry grin, 'Well, you didn't actually.'

With their wartime differences behind them, the two men and two other officers talked about the ramming incident as if it had been a football match. The Engineer Officer then escorted George to the quarterdeck. Here he was shown a piece of the *Proteus*'s port forward hydroplane, the one which had broken off and stuck inside the destroyer. The fragment had been mounted on a small plaque and was on display on the quarterdeck. It had a notice underneath it stating that the hydroplane was from a submarine which they had sunk. The men then sealed the occasion with a drink and expressions of goodwill.

George left the Mediterranean and sailed the *Ultor* to Gibraltar, the gateway to the Med. He was particularly interested to see the American naval 'blimps' flying sedately overhead while on patrol to guard the Strait of Gibraltar. From there, *Ultor* joined a convoy and made her way back to the United Kingdom.

While on passage to the United Kingdom, on 16 August 1944, the Admiralty summarized the exploits of *Ultor*'s fifteenth Mediterranean patrol and presented them to the Navy Board.

Lieutenant Hunt has the truly remarkable record of having achieved hits with almost fifty percent of torpedoes fired by him. The brilliance of his attacks on the 27th June are … unsurpassed in the annals of the Mediterranean Submarine Flotillas. His second attack, carried out from inside the screen against a tanker with nine surface and five aircraft escorts, overwhelming odds in favour of the enemy, was pressed home to succeed with great gallantry and consummate skill. It is quite clear … that not only Lieutenant Hunt, but his officers and the whole of his ship's company have achieved and maintained a degree of efficiency which reflects the highest credit on all of them. Lieutenant Hunt's own performance ... must entitle him to be classed with our front-rank Submarine Commanding Officers.

CHAPTER TWENTY-ONE

Home

The *Ultor* arrived back in the United Kingdom in early September 1944. Luckily for George, the convoy was directed to return to Scotland. It was a proud moment as the *Ultor* arrived at the Holy Loch on the Firth of Clyde, downriver from Glasgow. As she secured alongside the depot ship, HMS *Forth*, George savoured the familiar sights of Scotland and the green hills rising behind the small coastal village. As he stood on the bridge, his boyhood dreams well and truly realized, waves of nostalgia passed over him – the Firth of Clyde had been one of his favourite sailing venues as a young man. He was welcomed by the Captain of HMS *Forth* and he and his crew boarded the depot ship. Here, cabins for the officers and mess decks, already allocated, awaited the crew.

From Holy Loch, George commanded the *Ultor* for the last time. He sailed the boat around the north of Scotland to Blyth in north-east England, where his next assignment was to be in command of HMS *Taku*.

Taku was a British T-class submarine which had been commissioned in 1940. She had also seen service in the Mediterranean and had been damaged by a mine in April earlier that same year, 1944. She was now being used as a training ship, allowing those on training classes to experience practical work at sea.

HMS *Taku* was a large and aesthetically beautiful boat. She had taken her name from a fort which had achieved notoriety during the Chinese Boxer Rebellion. The regular submarine training unit was at Portsmouth in the south of England, but as it had been considered a little too close physically to the enemy, shore training had been moved to Blyth. George looked forward to the challenges.

At Blyth, George handed the *Ultor* over to another Captain and the crew were disbanded – it was a poignant moment for them all. As a team, they had experienced and survived many dangerous and nerve-racking situations.

During the previous two years, they lived, fought and slept together side by side. During that time, they had only three changes of personnel, one of which was a good cook. After *Ultor*, some moved to different ships and on to other naval careers, but most stayed on with the *Ultor*, under a different Captain. They all vowed to keep in touch.

When George reported, in due course, to the Admiral commanding submarines in London, he asked George, 'What about your wife? She's a Wren, isn't she?'

'She's at HMS *Glendower* in Wales, Sir. She didn't know exactly when I'd be returning,' George replied.

HMS *Glendower* was actually an old holiday camp destination – a Butlins, which had been requisitioned to train up to 1,000 sailors for the Normandy landings. Phoebe, who was a Chief Wren Regulating, was responsible for 200 Wrens there. With a big grin, she later admitted to George that her hardest job was to keep the Wrens away from the sailors.

The Admiral sent a signal to HMS *Glendower.* 'I should be grateful if you would arrange a transfer for Chief Petty Officer Wren Hunt to HMS *Calliope.*' HMS *Calliope* was a naval base in North Shields, just south of Blyth at the mouth of the Tyne River.

Phoebe was transferred almost immediately. On her arrival in Blyth, the couple had a marvellous reunion and, on 12 September, went on leave to Moffat in Scotland, where George's aunts lived. George and Phoebe had been separated for twenty-one months and they had missed each other terribly. They had written as often as they could but each was anxious for the other. Both had duties to attend to and this they did in the best traditions of war service. They returned from leave on 24 October and, a few days later, George assumed command of HMS *Taku*. In the meantime, Phoebe was able to commute daily to HMS *Calliope* just a short distance away.

George was happy for the quieter life here. As already described, his job was predominantly to take the training class to sea each day for practical experience. He enjoyed it and it allowed him to relax.

The couple lived in comfortable 'digs' in Blyth and greatly appreciated being together again. They were looked after by an attentive elderly lady who fed them and insisted on looking after everything: washing, bed-making (an enormous feather bed) and housekeeping. George adapted well to the transition to 'normal' Navy life.

As part of the reward for his Mediterranean service, George was awarded a year's seniority from September 1944, an accolade he was happy to accept.

Several special events highlighted the next few months, November being particularly interesting. On the first of that month, George was thrilled to receive accelerated promotion to the rank of Lieutenant Commander, a rare privilege for someone of only 28.

Other high distinctions came his way. For his courage and skill in command of the *Ultor*, he was appointed a Companion of the Distinguished Service Order (DSO). The moment was even sweeter as Barry Rowe was awarded a Distinguished Service Cross (DSC) and eleven of his crew were awarded Distinguished Service Medals (DSM). Eleven were also awarded Mentions in Dispatches (MiDs). In a rare event, because of *Ultor*'s record, King George VI expressed a wish for those receiving medals to all attend together (thirteen of them), for the one investiture. Normally, the protocol for decorating officers and ratings (other ranks) was that each attended separate investitures.

The ceremony was held at Buckingham Palace on 7 November 1944 and was also attended by Phoebe and all the crewmen's wives. It was a proud and memorable occasion, with the pinnacle being an insightful address by the King, who offered sincere congratulations to them all on an outstanding effort. It was particularly pleasing for George as the King stressed the need for teamwork as an integral ingredient to their success.

George was always very aware that in a submarine, even though the Captain is the individual who looks through the periscope and ultimately makes the decisions, he is reliant on individuals and cell groups spread throughout the submarine at action stations, and on their ability to respond instantly and cohesively. In fact, George considered that the Captain simply runs a well-trained team, many of whom he can't see, but is nevertheless absolutely dependent on them. The success of a submarine does indeed rely on good teamwork.

Sweetening the occasion, the local newspaper in Moffat, Dumfriesshire, reported George as a 'Submarine Commander of unsurpassed brilliance'.

On 14 November, all of the *Ultor*'s company were invited to Radcliffe, a town not far from Manchester. During the war, various towns adopted a ship (or a battalion or squadron) and raised money to assist their Canteen Fund. Committees became very enthusiastic in this endeavour and during their service in the Mediterranean, Radcliffe had supported the *Ultor*.

The Mayor received George and his crew, and laid on a civic reception for them. During the ceremony, George handed over *Ultor*'s prized Jolly Roger for safe-keeping in the town museum. In return, he was presented with the City's Coat of Arms. (Radcliffe is now assimilated into the larger metropolis of Bury.)

(Even though each submarine kept a Jolly Roger itself, maintained by the signalman, his needlecraft was often rough and ready. The owner of one of the finest lace shops in Malta, Carmela Cassar, arranged for the nuns to make beautifully embroidered Jolly Rogers, each about 12 by 18 inches, with a realistic skull and crossbones and all the exploits to which a particular submarine was entitled. *Ultor*'s silk Jolly Roger, made by the nuns, is now in a framed glass display at the Submarine Museum in Gosport, near Portsmouth.)

On 5 December, George received his final official accolade when he was awarded a bar to his DSO. The citation reads: 'For outstanding courage, skill and determination shown when in command of His Majesty's Submarine *Ultor* in a daring attack pressed home on strongly escorted enemy ships on 27th June 1944.' On 27 February 1945, George attended another investiture at Buckingham Palace to receive this award. This, for George, completed a remarkable series of awards as follows:

January 1941 –	Mentioned in Dispatches (MiD) for his bravery and leadership during the *Unity* sinking.
June 1942 –	Distinguished Service Cross (DSC) when First Lieutenant in the *Proteus*, and for his actions when *Proteus* was rammed by an Italian destroyer.
February 1944 –	Bar to DSC – when in command of *Ultor*.
May 1944 –	Mentioned in Dispatches (MiD) – for beach-marking in the Anzio landings.
September 1944 –	Distinguished Service Order (DSO) – when in command of *Ultor*.
December 1944 –	Bar to DSO – for the attacks on 27 June 1944 when in command of *Ultor*.

To receive these four medals, George and Phoebe attended three investitures at the Palace: July 1942, November 1944 (with his crew members) and February 1945. Overall, the Captain and crew of the *Ultor* achieved a fine record of awards: two DSOs, three DSCs, eleven DSMs and thirteen MiDs.

In April 1945, George's career took a different turn. As has been mentioned, he had been promoted to Lieutenant Commander and would be leaving submarines temporarily to do his 'Big Ship' time. He was selected to attend a staff course followed by a tactical course at the Royal Naval College, Greenwich, in preparation for a stint with aircraft carriers. After seven years continuously living and working with submarines, George needed to be brought up to date with matters concerning the rest of the Navy, and, of course, aircraft carriers.

Greenwich is a pleasant place on the Thames and George (with Phoebe) settled into life as a student again. The Royal Naval Staff College is an exquisite building, commissioned by Henry VIII as his Palace, right on the river. It had beautiful oak floors, a lecture hall, a large chapel, a special room under the chapel where Henry had built a 9-pin bowling alley, and a marvellous dining hall with an erotically painted ceiling covered with naked females. One of George's friends testified he actually counted over six hundred breasts.

While at the Staff College, George was honoured to be one of two submariners selected by the Admiralty to have his portrait painted for the Imperial War Museum. The other officer was Lieutenant L.W.A. Bennington, the Captain of HMS *Tally Ho* – the submarine which Phoebe had launched at Vickers shipbuilders at Barrow in Furness on 23 December 1942 (which also happened to be her birthday). The painting was completed by the celebrated Official War Artist, Anthony Devas. George sat for the portrait five times and was pleased with the end result. (The painting is in the Imperial War Museum, London, to this day.)

George had not been at Greenwich long, when, on 8 May, news was announced that the war in Europe was over – VE Day. He could hear the sounds of great excitement echoing from London – people cheering and celebrating as well as sirens and the tooting of ships' horns on the River Thames. Unfortunately, there were to be no official celebrations for the officers of the Staff College – the Navy was still technically at war.

George was in class when the news came through and the Director entered and said, 'Well, it's good news, but I'm sorry to tell you that we can't celebrate today. As you realise, we are to have a lecture this morning on the Far East, Burma and the Pacific. The war isn't over for us yet. Most of you will be going to fight the Japanese, so you'd better be paying attention – we won't be celebrating VE day here. Sorry about that!'

So the class pressed on with the lecture. For ordinary Londoners, however, the news was marvellous and celebrations could be heard going on day and night.

After the staff course, George continued studying. This mainly took the form of many short courses, such as fire-fighting, ship stability, tactical lessons and radar. This included a month's course on amphibious warfare at Camberley, the Army Staff College.

In August 1945, George joined his next ship, a brand-new aircraft carrier, HMS *Triumph*. The *Triumph* was a Colossus-class light fleet carrier and had only been launched in October 1944 by Lady Louis Mountbatten. It had been built by Hawthorn Leslie and Company on the Tyne and was due to be commissioned into the Royal Navy in mid-1946, so George was due to go on several courses in preparation for this event.

On an aircraft carrier, the Captain is Captain of the ship. The Commander is Second-in-Command of the ship and four other commanders look after aircraft (thirty-six of them in this case), engines, electronic instruments and supply. As First Lieutenant, George was to be responsible for all the 'seamanship' side of the carrier – boats, anchors, cables, mooring and replenishment at sea. In action, however, he would preside in the Damage Control Headquarters. His main responsibilities were, of course, damage control, which also embraces fire-fighting and the stability of the ship.

Even though many aspects of commanding and running a carrier were decidedly different to those of a submarine, George relished the challenges and enjoyed this build-up. Although he didn't have to be involved with the aircraft to any great extent, he was delighted to fly as a passenger several times, and relished the experience and adrenalin of taking off and landing on the carrier.

In mid-August, news came through that the second atom bomb had been dropped in Japan on Nagasaki and Japan had surrendered. The war was over. At the time, George was doing a 'Damage Control Course' at the Royal Naval Barracks in Portsmouth. He reacted like everybody else to the finish of the war – there was great excitement and relief, with the general sentiment: 'Thank God they've dropped the bomb. There'll be no more killing.' There was no debate about the morality or rights or wrongs of the bombing. It was very clear no more men or women would be sacrificed. It was finished.

For George, this ended six long years of war in which he had carried out thirty-two operational patrols, seventeen of them in *Ultor*.

With the war finally ended, the submarine officers held a special 'Victory Reunion' on 31 January 1946, in HMS *Dolphin* (the Alma Mater of British and many Commonwealth submarine officers). Many Allied officers were also invited. George attended the gathering, during which the officers were called upon to drink the time-honoured toast to the more than 8,700 officers and men who had lost their lives – a very moving moment.

In the meantime, the other important news for George and Phoebe was the impending birth of their child. In March 1946, George was at Hawthorn Leslie, shipbuilders on the River Tyne in the north-east of England, 'standing by' and waiting for the builders of *Triumph* to hand the ship over to the Navy. Phoebe's time was 'close' and George decided, 'The baby has to be born in Scotland!' So Phoebe was transferred, as previously arranged, to Edinburgh, and was welcomed into the care of very old friends: a doctor and his wife. Here, their daughter, Susan, was born on 16 April.

George was at sea at the time. *Triumph* had been commissioned on 9 April and was undergoing final sea trials. She had just berthed at Rosyth on the Firth of Forth, not far from Edinburgh, when George received a telegram announcing Susan's birth. He immediately travelled to where she was born in Randolph Crescent – a wonderful moment after all the years of war. Not only was it fantastic to see his darling Phoebe and her baby, but he felt that now, at last, the baby would never have to experience the horrors of war.

The *Triumph* was eventually accepted by the Navy (after trials) on 6 May 1946.

The following month, throughout the country, major centres were hosting parades to officially celebrate the end of the war. As the Navy is the Senior Service, members of HMS *Triumph* were given the honour of leading the Victory Parade and George was to lead the ship's company through the streets of Southampton, which meant that he would be leading the entire parade. As well as the Navy, Army and Air Force, this consisted of civilian forces such as firefighters, ambulance personnel, police and others, not forgetting 'Dad's Army', the Home Guard. For some days he practised marching on the deck of the *Triumph* with his sword drawn. The actual event was a proud moment, but there were elements of drama and humour involved.

Two policemen mounted on loud, revving motorbikes preceded George. Besides the danger of becoming poisoned from their exhaust fumes, the bikes were so noisy George couldn't hear the band – the

155

officer marching behind him was therefore deputized to call out the beat so George could stay in step.

Apart from that minor challenge, the parade was a great success in all other ways and served to help the community achieve a form of closure.

For the last six years, the nation and individuals had been placed under tremendous pressure, often leading to great public and personal loss, devastation and upheaval. They had endured severe rationing of food and all resources, blackouts, bombings, land-mines, air-raid shelters and family separations, and had suffered many other losses. This event was therefore a formal attempt to come to terms with the circumstances of the past and the start of rebuilding for the future.

To finish off a memorable and happy 'end-of-war feeling', George, Phoebe and their daughter Susan attended a garden party at Buckingham Palace and 'had tea with the King and Queen'. There were about a hundred other people at the event and the three of them found the occasion both moving and fascinating.

It was time to move on.

Epilogue

The After Years – What Happened to George After the War?

George's continued life story makes for compelling reading, completing a fulfilling chronicle of exploration, enterprise and achievement.

After the Victory Parade in Southampton in June 1946, George remained as First Lieutenant of HMS *Triumph* until early the next year. One of the highlights of this time concerns an experience when the *Triumph* was selected, as the newest aircraft carrier, to transport the First Sea Lord, Admiral Sir Bruce Fraser, to Russia to receive an award, the Order of Suvorov. *Triumph* was to go to Kronstadt, an old Russian naval base in the Gulf of Finland in the Baltic Sea. From there, Sir Bruce would continue travelling up the Neva to St Petersburg, then on to Moscow. It was still dangerous times and territory as, while approaching Kronstadt, one of the Russian minesweepers, while sweeping a safe passage for the *Triumph* to enter Kronstadt, hit a mine and was seriously damaged.

Before he left for Moscow, Sir Bruce discussed his return with the Captain of *Triumph*. He then tested George's abilities as an 'events co-ordinator'.

'When I get back,' he said, 'I'll have some high-ranking Russian officials with me. I'm going to give a dinner on the quarterdeck and I want you to take charge of the arrangements.'

157

This was a massive exercise in logistics. To begin with, the 'built-in' tables in the Officers' Wardroom had to be sawn in half to get them out. They then had to be manhandled up the gangway and rebuilt on the quarterdeck. This entailed the co-ordination of shipwrights and sailors initially, followed by discussions with the Supply Department, Royal Marines and other departments.

After overcoming a number of problems, the actual event was deemed a great success. The after-dinner entertainment began with the Russians rendering a stirring Cossack song. At the request of the Admiral, George was given the opportunity to perform. He asked a Royal Marine bandsman to play a particular bagpipe tune on a violin and then proceeded to execute a competent Scottish sword dance. Sir Bruce, who was also a Scot, was most impressed and said to him, 'You do the sword dance well.'

'I enjoy it, Sir.'

'Well done.' He smiled and went on, 'It impressed the Russians.'

George stayed with the *Triumph* until February 1947. When he was reappointed to submarines, he requalified and refreshed his commanding officer and technical skills by doing the 'Perisher' Course again at HMS *Dolphin* in Portsmouth. In March, he took command of another submarine, HMS *Ambush*. Later that year, in October, Phoebe and young Susan flew by flying boat to South Africa to visit her family – a novel experience at that time. In November George had a memorable, and unnerving, experience. He carried out a series of trials under the ice in and around the Arctic Ocean. These were largely aimed at monitoring the underside of the icecap, using an inverted echo-sounder. George continued on with *Ambush* until January 1948.

His next appointment was for almost three years as Commanding Officer of the COs' Qualifying Course, a position known as 'Teacher-Captain of the Perisher'. While there, in June 1948, George was promoted to Commander at the age of 31. This was a great honour as the CO and Chief Instructor of the course had a heavy responsibility. The course was based from the depot ship HMS *Montclare* at Rothesay Bay, in the Firth of Clyde. Most of this time was spent at sea, taking his class of four or five aspiring Captains out in a submarine. A great deal of the time was spent carrying out attacks, firing actual practice torpedoes and simulating war conditions.

The particular submarine that had been allocated for the three-month courses came complete with its own Captain and crew, and was temporarily known as the 'Perisher Boat'. There were many minor 'incidents' involving the students, particularly as they became confused while acting as 'Captain for the day'.

In August 1949, George finally received his '28 days end-of-war leave', which he spent in Norway. One of George's great friends, with whom he had served during the war, 'Ronnie' Ronneburg, a Norwegian submarine captain who had married a British Wren officer, invited George, Phoebe and Susan over to Norway for the holiday. The Ronneburgs' little daughter Pookie was the same age as Susan (3) and they got on famously together.

Ronneburg's uncle owned a cabin up in the mountains beside a lake. The setting was idyllic. Both families spent much of the time together, mainly fishing for trout and exploring, for three weeks. It was a marvellous wind-down.

After the holiday, George continued in his position as Teacher-Captain of the COs' Qualifying Course until May 1950, when he became Operations Officer on Flag Officer Submarines Staff at HMS *Dolphin*.

In 1952, he left the Staff and was moved back to aircraft carriers. Here, as a Commander, he was appointed Second-in-Command and Executive Officer of HMS *Theseus* and was accountable for virtually everything to the Captain. It was a significant responsibility as an aircraft carrier is effectively a floating town with (then) 1,500 inhabitants.

Theseus, at that time, was the Mediterranean Fleet Flagship for Admiral Lord Louis Mountbatten, the Commander-in-Chief, Mediterranean Fleet. This was a busy period with Fleet exercises, earthquake relief and Fleet visits – 'showing the flag' – on the agenda. George revisited Greece as major earthquakes had recently devastated regions of Greece and Cyprus, the most desperate region being Paphos, at the southern end of Cyprus. *Theseus* assisted with food, shelter and medical relief for the damaged village.

Another highlight was a State Visit by the Fleet to Istanbul to celebrate the 500th anniversary of the taking of Constantinople by the Ottoman Turks. Lord Louis gave a reception on the flight deck of *Theseus* for 750 guests, including the President of Turkey. The Royal Marines 'beat retreat' on the flight deck and at the end of the ceremonial, the President presented a pair of beautiful silver cymbals to the Royal Marine Bandmaster. In doing so, he made the point that cymbals originated in Turkey.

George was largely responsible to his Captain for the organization and running of this function, and even though it tested his organizational skills somewhat, and those of his splendid team, he was pleased when the occasion was deemed a great success. Another pleasing aspect of his time on *Theseus* concerned the volunteer Band. George was a member of the Royal Naval Pipers Society, and with the blessing of the Captain, Captain Russell, a fellow Scot, he managed to augment the Band with four pipers from the ship's company.

In June 1953, HMS *Theseus* took part in the very impressive Royal Fleet Review in the Solent, to mark the Coronation of HM Queen Elizabeth II. Both George and his Captain, Douglas Russell, were awarded the Queen's Coronation Medal, an occasion of great pageantry and pride.

The same year saw both some sadness and another highlight. First, George's mother died in Scotland and was cremated in Edinburgh, creating a significant loss. However, the high watermark was his promotion to Captain, at the age of 37, an honour in itself. As Admiral S.M. Raw noted in his congratulatory letter, he was the 'youngest of the batch'. George was particularly pleased to receive a letter of congratulations from the Commander-in-Chief, Mediterranean, Lord Mountbatten. It was signed personally, 'Yours very Sincerely, Mountbatten of Burma'.

As such, in January 1954, George took command of HM Underwater Detection Establishment at Portland, Dorset, back in England. This was a large naval facility with seven assorted trials craft under his command. Phoebe was able to live with him in a beautiful 200-year-old house, Burgundy House, and while there her parents came over on a visit from South Africa.

The Underwater Detection Establishment concentrated on the development of new and better types of Asdic/sonar equipment. The work was highly technical and George, with the Chief Scientist, had a great number of scientists (who were officers in the Royal Naval Scientific Service) and eight naval officers, working on refinements. It was a most interesting period and very rewarding.

In June 1955, while in Portland, George became significantly involved in the aftermath of a tragic event which occurred in Portland Harbour. The depot ship, HMS *Maidstone*, was secured to a buoy in the harbour with several submarines berthed alongside her. At the time, George could see all the ships in the harbour from the windows of his office and noticed some sort of disturbance. One of the submarines, HMS *Sidon*, was preparing for sea, when suddenly an explosion shook the boat. This was followed by a tremendous rush of air shooting up through the conning tower. The detonation had been caused by one of the torpedoes' hydrogen peroxide propellant (HTP), which had started to flow out of its containers. HTP was an unstable and dangerous substance.

Because the torpedo was in the confined space of its tube, and both the bow cap and rear door were shut, the extreme heat and pressure, combined with the volatility of HTP, simply climaxed in an explosion. This blasted the rear door of the tube open and blew off the bow cap. Sea water immediately raced straight into the submarine, which started to sink by the bow. Tragically, three officers and ten ratings lost their lives.

As George was a submariner and available locally, he was appointed officially to convene a Board of Enquiry which was held on board HMS *Maidstone*. The findings of the Board, put simply, reinforced the decision not to proceed further with HTP. (The Royal Navy had been trialling HTP since the 'capture' of the German U-boat *U1407* at the end of the war.) As a result, the Royal Navy and the United States Navy, both of which had closely followed the trials in the Royal Navy, decided against its further use. (Russia, however, was determined to go its own way and continued to pursue the use of HTP in torpedoes. The tragic result was the total loss of the Russian submarine *Kursk* in August 2000, including 118 officers and men.)

George commanded the Underwater Detection Establishment for two years until January 1956. From there, he was appointed Captain of HMS *Bigbury Bay*, a Bay-class anti-submarine frigate and the Seventh Frigate Squadron. Then, upgraded to the rank of Commodore, he took *Bigbury Bay* to Bermuda where he relieved the Commander-in-Chief, Vice Admiral Sir Jack Eaton, and became Senior Naval Officer West Indies (SNOWI). He was also appointed in a NATO capacity as 'Island Commander Bermuda'. This, of course, was a military appointment, and had nothing to do with the actual government of Bermuda.

In those days, the rank of Commodore, in both the Royal Navy and the United States Navy, was a special temporary appointment prior to filling a higher post. In this case, George was to take over from a Vice Admiral and assume command of a slightly reduced naval station as Senior Naval Officer West Indies. He could expect to revert to Captain at the end of that appointment. (Today, Commodore is mainly a step in rank achieved by some Captains to fill certain NATO and kindred jobs, and important naval positions in the normal way.)

George's area of responsibility was vast. He was accountable to the Admiralty for Royal Navy interests from the Amazon in South America to the Canadian border, and west to the Panama Canal. As such, his squadron undertook many joint exercises with the US Navy, the Dutch from the Netherlands Antilles and the French in Martinique.

Even though this was primarily a seagoing appointment, George was allowed to have his family with him, arranged officially by the Navy. Phoebe and Susan therefore went to Bermuda and Susan attended school there. It was a very busy period for George as Britain had fifteen colonies in the area. Governors and administrators who ran these colonies occasionally had disturbances.

Because of incipient problems in the region, Britain maintained a brigadier in Jamaica, with a battalion of the Duke of Cornwall's

Light Infantry. On one occasion, George had to move them to a particular island during a period of social unrest, while on two others it was sufficient just to 'show the flag'. During these minor 'troubles', he simply arrived by ship and landed a party of sailors.

The first such occasion was to British Honduras (now modern-day Belize), and the other to Nassau in the Bahamas, following specific requests by the respective Governors for assistance. This was always a tricky situation and came under the heading 'Aid to the Civil Power'. Such assistance required a direct request from the Governor and, of course, a very close working relationship with the local police.

In essence, George would normally land a party of sailors, with the First Lieutenant in command. Their main function was to guard key places such as Government House, important buildings and vulnerable points (VPs), particularly the Cable and Wireless Company interchange station, telephone exchange and the airport. The sailors, when landed, wore military belts, gaiters and 'tin hats', and were armed with rifles and bayonets; they always 'looked the part', instilling the situation with some authority.

On both occasions, the 'troubles' subsided and ended, in the case of Belize, with a cricket match between the sailors and the locals, including some who had caused the disturbance in the first place.

An interesting highlight for George occurred in 1957 when he took HMS *Bigbury Bay* right up the James River to Jamestown in Virginia, to represent the Royal Navy at the 350th anniversary celebrations of the landing of the first English settlers. While there, Sir Harold Caccia, the British Ambassador to the USA, gave a reception on his ship for President Eisenhower.

Another high point for George was taking his ship to Annapolis, the college for midshipmen and the 'cradle of the United States Navy'. The Commandant of the College, Rear Admiral William R. Smedberg III, asked George if he would like his two National Service midshipmen to stay on in the College. It was a nice gesture. While in Annapolis, George was fascinated to see the sarcophagus enclosing the remains of John Paul Jones, the famous American naval officer and 'founder' of the US Navy. George was particularly interested as Jones had been a Scot, born in Kirkcudbright, Dumfriesshire (about 70 kilometres from Moffat) and had emigrated to America.

On another occasion, George took *Bigbury Bay* for an interesting visit to Cuba where they paraded the White Ensign and George laid a wreath. However, more importantly, his ship was very well received by the Cuban Navy and many local dignitaries, especially Admiral Calderon, the Chief of the Navy. Accompanied by the British Ambassador, His Excellency Mr A.S. Fordham, George paid an official call on President Batista. About two weeks later, President Batista fled the country and Fidel Castro took over.

Bermuda was chosen as the venue for an important meeting between Sir Harold Macmillan, Prime Minister of the United Kingdom, President Eisenhower of the United States, and Mr Diefenbaker, Prime Minister of Canada. Their discussions included the supply of Polaris missiles to the United Kingdom for nuclear deterrent submarines, among other things. George was responsible, together with Bermuda's Police Chief, for general security, but particularly for the Mid Ocean Golf Club House, the actual venue of the meeting. Before departing, however, the three celebrities gave a dinner party for the Governor and other Bermudan authorities, and included George, Phoebe and two of *Bigbury Bay*'s officers.

In June 1957, *Bigbury Bay* left Bermuda to return to the United Kingdom for her refit. HMS *Troubridge* had arrived two months previously and now HMS *Ulster* joined the squadron fresh from Britain. Having two ships certainly eased the pressure, especially concerning the new business of the drugs scene, and the extra work involved – not to mention the exercises, flag-showing and ceremonial connected with various functions.

One particular episode was the 'Federation of the West Indies'. The premiers of the various main islands decided to 'federate' under the British flag. Lord Hailes, the British Minister for Works, was to be the first Governor General of the Federation and this involved transporting Lord and Lady Hailes, and their immediate staff, to visit each main island, a task that was undertaken mainly by HMS

Troubridge.

Finally, in April 1958, George and his squadron were very involved in the ceremonies and celebrations in Port of Spain, Trinidad, at the time of the inauguration of the Federation. The celebration started with his sailors street-lining the route and mounting a Guard of Honour for the arrival of Princess Margaret. At the same time, HMS *Ulster* fired a Royal gun salute. Of great assistance in all this ceremonial was HMS *Vidal. Vidal* wasn't part of the squadron, but was involved in carrying out hydrographic surveys in the West Indies, and of course was able to assist.

All of this preceded the actual ceremony to install Lord Hailes as Governor General, and a speech by Princess Margaret. This was followed by a lavish lunch at which George sat across the table from Princess Margaret – in all, a most memorable occasion. (Four years after the Federation was inaugurated in 1962, the islands decided to dismantle the Federation and go it alone, many to become completely independent.)

While in this appointment, much of George's time was spent in taking his ships on 'Showing the Flag' visits, exercises with other navies and as 'hurricane guardship' duties. During this time, a particularly sinister episode occurred as the development of the drugs trade started to raise its ugly head; when requested, some of George's ships carried out searches of suspected cays. On one such occasion, George received a signal instructing him to land a party and search Cay Sal (Salt Cay), a small uninhabited island. The secret signal said that drugs had been buried there, but where exactly?

The *Bigbury Bay* duly anchored off the island and a large party of sailors, all keen to enjoy a banyan party, stretch their legs and have a swim, went ashore and diligently searched acres of beach without success. This was very early in the drug business and the first time the Navy had been instructed to carry out a search. However, a good time was enjoyed by all except for some cases of sunburn.

George's service in the West Indies was one of the most interesting, exciting and challenging of his career. When many colonies (not only British ones) were becoming independent, it might be interesting to note that Bermuda, which was certainly one of

Britain's very oldest colonies, held a referendum and voted overwhelmingly to remain a colony just two or three years after George left.

In 1958, George, reverting in rank from Commodore back to Captain, returned to the United Kingdom with his family and rejoined Flag Officer Submarines Staff, this time as the Chief Staff Officer. In June 1959, when HM the Queen presented her Colour to the Submarine Command, George and Phoebe were honoured to be presented to Her Majesty.

An interesting experience for George at this time was to have a spell at sea in USS *Skipjack*, one of the United States Navy's new nuclear submarines. What a difference the submarine of the future, a world away from his *Ultor*.

A pleasing incident for George while in the post was that he was invited to present the prizes at the end of term at his old Alma Mater, HMS *Conway* – the wheel had turned full circle.

George's last three years in the Royal Navy comprised an appointment to the Admiralty offices in Bath, in 1960. For many years, the more technical departments of the Admiralty, such as ship construction, dockyards, refitting and engineering had been moved from London to this ancient Roman city. George found Bath interesting as hot springs still poured out of lead piping into baths built by the Romans.

He was appointed Director of Naval Equipment, working with several directors of other departments, all under Sir Alfred Sims, the Director General Ships. George had a staff of eight naval officers and, aided by them, he was responsible for, among other things, the inspections and acceptance trials of every submarine, and certain surface ships, being built around the country. His team worked very closely with the Royal Corps of Naval Constructors and with the Principal Naval Overseers in each dockyard.

George also worked closely with the Commodore Superintendent of Contract-Built Ships (surface warships) because he was responsible for improving habitability aboard ships and replenishment at sea. This role applied equally to submarines and surface ships. He soon discovered that his job (which was, for obvious reasons, invariably held by a submariner), Director of Naval Equipment, also covered other interesting and rewarding functions. He was Chairman of the Standing Committee on Submarine Escape, entailing close ties with the Royal Naval Physiological Laboratory, and trials in the 100-foot (32-metre) escape training tank, as well as at sea in submarines. He was also Chairman of the Royal Naval Life Saving Committee, which encompassed live trials of volunteers in life-rafts in mid-Atlantic, immersion suits in the Arctic, ordinary life jackets, Antarctic inflating rafts, distress signals, flares, dye, smoke and even shark repellents for naval divers.

Yet another of his absorbing roles was Chairman of the Ships, Badges and Names Committee, which included the College of Heralds among its members. The naming of the bigger ships was normally submitted to the reigning monarch through the Admiralty for approval, and many of the old names were re-used where appropriate.

Finally, since he had been heavily involved with HMS *Dreadnought*, the Royal Navy's first nuclear submarine, George and Phoebe were present when she was launched by the Queen. They were also invited to lunch on board HM Royal Yacht *Britannia* by the Commanding Officer of the Yacht.

In 1963, at the age of 46, it became time for George to contemplate his future in the Navy. He had risen to the top of the 'Captain's List' and the next step would be promotion to Rear Admiral – or retirement. There were a number of things to be considered. Firstly, at that time, there was to be a reduction in the size of the Fleet and, as such, a reduction in the number of Flag Officers. If he remained in the Navy, because of his record he would have been selected for further commands at sea, something that impacted on his final decision. During twenty years of married life, he had only experienced one appointment in which he could have his family with him while overseas.

A year or so earlier, it had been decreed that in future, when officers were promoted to Commander or Captain, they would be put on a 'Post List' or 'Dry List'. Those on the Post List could reasonably expect further sea time and commands at sea, while those on the Dry List would expect important staff appointments and perhaps NATO or similar jobs. This, unfortunately, created some uncertainty, and officers who had set their heart on commanding ships but who then found themselves on the Dry List did, in one or two cases, actually resign.

George, who was on the Post List, was beginning to hope for more time to enjoy and be with his family – one of the many items to be considered in this great and important decision. He felt if he left the Navy *now* he could look forward to at least another fifteen years of meaningful work which he would *not* get by staying in the Navy, even if promoted to Admiral. Furthermore, it would be easier to find a job aged 46 as a Captain, than try to find a job as an Admiral in his fifties. In addition, Susan was now about to leave school and go to university or find a job. In the end, it was a family decision – they decided it would be better to start afresh in a new country.

And so, having commanded seven ships, including five submarines, and having completed ten years as a Captain, three years of which was as a Commodore, with great regret, George retired from the Royal Navy. He was, however, recognized by the Registrar General of Shipping and Seamen in the United Kingdom and granted a Foreign-Going Master's Certificate enabling him to command a merchant ship. This was an internationally recognized certificate.

It was time for George and Phoebe to make a decision on where to settle. George had lived a great deal of his life in tropical climes, beginning with his early childhood in Uganda. His pre-war naval exploits had been around the Orient, Asia and the Mediterranean, and Phoebe was from South Africa. As much as George loved Scotland, the couple decided they would go somewhere semi-tropical, in the sun. They chose Australia.

So, early that same year, 1963, George and his family sailed for South Africa, on their way to Australia, to be reunited with members of Phoebe's family. Sadly, Phoebe's father died on the very day they arrived in Cape Town.

The next two months were spent in South Africa helping Phoebe's mother, in Natal, with the funeral of her father, and catching up with other family and friends from other parts of South Africa. It turned out to be a lovely holiday for George, Phoebe and Susan, staying up in the Natal National Park, visiting friends in what was then Basutoland, going to the Kruger National park (Game Reserve) and camping out in their caravan. Then, finally, after seeing Phoebe's mother installed in a retirement village in Natal, they flew from Johannesburg to Mauritius.

From there, the family flew in a small Electra aircraft to the Cocos Islands where they were able to shower and have breakfast. Having freshened up, they boarded another plane to Australia and finally landed in Perth on 19 May 1963. Here, the family stayed with a cousin of friends from Moffat.

They liked Perth, which was having its wettest May in fifty years, to the extent that the water catchment at Mundaring Weir overflowed, resulting in considerable delays as they crossed the Nullarbor Plain by rail on the way to Adelaide. Parts of the line were washed away, both on the way to Kalgoorlie and on the Nullarbor itself. From Adelaide they pressed on to the 'Sunshine State' of Queensland.

With the family settled in Brisbane, George joined the staff at Evans Deakin's shipyard. He already had a Master's Certificate, so he obtained his Principal-in-Charge Certificate for the Brisbane River and took a number of newly-built smaller vessels out on trials, although he was mainly in charge of naval repairs and special projects.

During this period, he and Phoebe became Australian citizens. Phoebe, meanwhile, became involved with the ex-Wrens Association and the two simply enjoyed their time together. Susan started work in the Queensland Book Depot and then spent about a year and a half working in New Zealand, staying briefly in Auckland with the Thodes (Con Thode and George had served together during the war). She also worked on sheep farms and in the ski resort of Queenstown on the South Island.

In 1965, the British High Commissioner to Australia, based in Canberra, the capital of Australia, travelled to Brisbane for a meeting. While there, he met and offered George a position in the

169

Diplomatic Service in Brisbane. George accepted and, after an interview, became a member of the British High Commission, working mainly on projects which were of importance to the Board of Trade in London. At the same time, he transferred to the Royal Australian Navy on the Emergency List, retaining his rank of Captain.

George continued working for the British High Commission in Brisbane for eleven years. It was very rewarding work and, to George, it was a most interesting time. The requirements involved travelling to many parts of Queensland, such as Weipa in the north, Longreach in the west and even occasionally over the border south to Grafton in New South Wales. Phoebe accompanied him on some of these long drives, the big open spaces reminding her of her girlhood in South Africa, especially the Karroo around Kimberley where she was born.

George retired in 1976, at the age of 60, and he and Phoebe built a small beach house at Toogoom, several hours' drive north of Brisbane. In the meantime, their daughter Susan had been working in Mines Administration in Brisbane, where she met and married Hedley Howard in 1969. During this period, Hedley was appointed Financial Controller of Magellan Petroleum Australia Limited. Their first child, Sarah Cecilia, was born in 1976 and their son, Alistair Scott, arrived in 1982. George and Phoebe spent six years at Toogoom and then returned to Brisbane in 1981, to be nearer Susan and her family. By this time Hedley was Managing Director of Magellan. Tragically, on the brink of retirement in 2001, Hedley died of cancer at the age of 59.

In 1989, George and Phoebe celebrated their Golden Wedding at the United Service Club in Brisbane and in 1990 they moved in to Forest Place Retirement Village at Durack, on the south side of Brisbane. Life was very good for them there until, in 2002, Phoebe fell and also suffered a stroke.

George lost his beloved Phoebe in August 2005, his dear companion of almost sixty-six years of marriage, a union that had continually set his seal for happiness. She died peacefully in her sleep, aged 89. It was a bitter blow to George and the family.

In 2006, to celebrate his 90th birthday, his still adventurous spirit was satisfied by a ride in a hot-air balloon with Susan, Sarah and Alistair, a birthday gift from the family. Indeed his daughter and grandchildren, all of whom lead very busy lives, mean a great deal to him and he treasures the times when he sees them.

At the time of writing, January 2010, George is now 94 and appears in generally good health. He is remarkably active and has a number of interests which take him to many official functions, particularly naval. He still communicates and corresponds with some of his old naval friends, including a few of his crew from the *Ultor*, something he enjoys and considers a great privilege.

George's many interests since coming to Australia in 1963 reflect his career in the Armed Forces and at sea, and they also express his commitment to his life in Australia. These include:

1965 – he joined the staff of the British High Commission in Brisbane.
1966 – he was elected President of the Royal United Service Institute, Queensland, and more recently he was made a Life Member.
1980 – he was made an Honorary Member of the United Service Club.
1994 – he was elected Patron of the Queensland Branch of the Submarine Association, and later, a Life Member of the Submarine Association of Australia.
1995 – he was made an Honorary Member of the Company of Master Mariners of Australia.

In addition, he received:

1993 – from Malta, the Malta George Cross 50th Anniversary Medal, 'Defence of Malta'.
1993 – from Greece, the Hellenic Republic Commemorative Medallion of Campaign 1941–1945, for actions in the Aegean.
1999 – from the Australian Merchant Navy Awards Council:

     – Commendation Medal for Service to Maritime Industry.
     – The Australian Merchant Navy Service Cross.
      In addition, he was interviewed officially for the 'Australians at War Film Archives' by the Government Archives team.

2005 – from Australian Government, Commemorative Medallion, 60th Anniversary of the end of the Second World War, 'For those who served'.

Of all the branches of men in the Forces, there is none which shows more devotion and faces grimmer perils than the submariners.

Winston S. Churchill, 1943

Select Bibliography

Baynham, B., *A Sailor's Life*, published privately.

Compton-Hall, R., *The Underwater War*, Blandford Press, Dorset, 1982.

Hay, I., *Malta*, London, Hodder & Stoughton Ltd, 1943.

Hezlet, A., *British and Allied Submarine Operations in World War II*, vol. I, The Royal Navy Submarine Museum, 2001.

Hood, J., *Submarine*, Conway, 2007.

Mackenzie, H., *The Sword of Damocles*, The Royal Navy Submarine Museum.

Spooner, T., *Supreme Gallantry: Malta's Role in the Allied Victory 1939–1945*, John Murray, London, 1996.

Wallace, R., *The Italian Campaign*, Time-Life Books, 1978.

Windsor, A., *HMS* Conway *1859–1974*, Witherby Steamship Company.

Wingate, J., *The Fighting Tenth*, Leo Cooper, London, 1991.